my **revisi**

EDEXCEL A2
GEOGRAPHY

Dan Cowling
Michael Witherick

HODDER
EDUCATION

Hodder Education, an Hachette UK company, 338 Euston Road, London NW1 3BH

Orders

Bookpoint Ltd, 130 Milton Park, Abingdon, Oxfordshire OX14 4SB
tel: 01235 827827
fax: 01235 400401
e-mail: education@bookpoint.co.uk
Lines are open 9.00 a.m.–5.00 p.m., Monday to Saturday, with a 24-hour message answering service. You can also order
through the Hodder Education website: www.hoddereducation.co.uk

First printed 2013
Impression number 5 4 3
Year 2017 2016 2015 2014

Cover photo reproduced by permission of Mopic/Fotolia. Photo on p.67 © Finnbarr Webster/Alamy

Typeset by Datapage (India) Pvt. Ltd.
Printed in India

Hachette UK's policy is to use papers that are natural, renewable and recyclable products and made from wood
grown in sustainable forests. The logging and manufacturing processes are expected to conform to the environmental
regulations of the country of origin.

P2190

Get the most from this book

Everyone has to decide his or her own revision strategy, but it is essential to review your work, learn it and test your understanding. These Revision Notes will help you to do that in a planned way, topic by topic. Use this book as the cornerstone of your revision and don't hesitate to write in it — personalise your notes and check your progress by ticking off each section as you revise.

☑ **Tick to track your progress**

Use the revision planner on pages 4 and 5 to plan your revision, topic by topic. Tick each box when you have:

● revised and understood a topic

● tested yourself

● practised the exam questions and gone online to check your answers and complete the quick quizzes

You can also keep track of your revision by ticking off each topic heading in the book. You may find it helpful to add your own notes as you work through each topic.

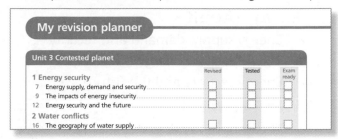

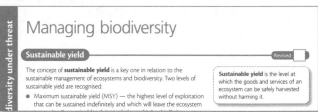

Features to help you succeed

Examiner's tips and summaries

Expert tips are given throughout the book to help you polish your exam technique in order to maximise your chances. The summaries provide a quick-check bullet list for each topic.

Typical mistakes

The authors identify the typical mistakes candidates make and explain how you can avoid them.

Revision activities

These activities will help you to understand each topic in an interactive way.

Now test yourself

These short, knowledge-based questions provide the first step in testing your learning.

Exam practice

Practice exam questions are provided for each topic. Use them to consolidate your revision and practise your exam skills.

Definitions and key words

Clear, concise definitions of essential key terms are provided on the page where they appear. Key words you need to know are highlighted in bold throughout the book.

Online

Go online to check your answers to the *Now test yourself* and *Exam practice* questions and try out the extra quick quizzes at:
www.therevisionbutton.co.uk/myrevisionnotes

My revision planner

Research options

You should choose one of the topics 8–13

	Revised	Tested	Exam ready

Now test yourself answers, Exam practice answers and quick quizzes online at
www.therevisionbutton.co.uk/myrevisionnotes

Countdown to my exams

6–8 weeks to go

- Start by looking at the specification — make sure you know exactly what material you need to revise and the style of the exam. Use the revision planner on pages 4 and 5 to familiarise yourself with the topics.
- Organise your notes, making sure you have covered everything on the specification. The revision planner will help you to group your notes into topics.
- Work out a realistic revision plan that will allow you time for relaxation. Set aside days and times for all the subjects that you need to study, and stick to your timetable.
- Set yourself sensible targets. Break your revision down into focused sessions of around 40 minutes, divided by breaks. These Revision Notes organise the basic facts into short, memorable sections to make revising easier.

Revised ☐

4–6 weeks to go

- Read through the relevant sections of this book and refer to the examiner's tips, examiner's summaries, typical mistakes and key terms. Tick off the topics as you feel confident about them. Highlight those topics you find difficult and look at them again in detail.
- Test your understanding of each topic by working through the 'Now test yourself' questions in the book. Look up the answers at **www. therevisionbutton.co.uk/myrevisionnotes**.
- Make a note of any problem areas as you revise, and ask your teacher to go over these in class.
- Look at past papers. They are one of the best ways to revise and practise your exam skills. Write or prepare planned answers to the exam practice questions provided in this book. Check your answers online and try out the extra quick quizzes at **www.therevisionbutton.co.uk/ myrevisionnotes**
- Try different revision methods. For example, you can make notes using mind maps, spider diagrams or flash cards.
- Track your progress using the revision planner and give yourself a reward when you have achieved your target.

Revised ☐

One week to go

- Try to fit in at least one more timed practice of an entire past paper and seek feedback from your teacher, comparing your work closely with the mark scheme.
- Check the revision planner to make sure you haven't missed out any topics. Brush up on any areas of difficulty by talking them over with a friend or getting help from your teacher.
- Attend any revision classes put on by your teacher. Remember, he or she is an expert at preparing people for examinations.

Revised ☐

The day before the examination

- Flick through these Revision Notes for useful reminders, for example the examiner's tips, examiner's summaries, typical mistakes and key terms.
- Check the time and place of your examination.
- Make sure you have everything you need — extra pens and pencils, tissues, a watch, bottled water, sweets.
- Allow some time to relax and have an early night to ensure you are fresh and alert for the examination.

Revised ☐

My exams

AS Geography Unit 3

Date: . . . .

Time: . . . .

Location:. . . . .

AS Geography Unit 4

Date: . . . .

Time: . . . .

Location:. . . . .

1 Energy security

Revised

Key concepts

There are three key concepts running through this topic: **energy**, **energy security** and **energy mix**. They need to be understood if you are to succeed in the forthcoming exam. So start your revision of this topic by double-checking that you have a sound grasp of these concepts.

The key question here concerns energy security: how 'energy secure' is today's world?

Revision activity

Create a two-column table. In column 1, list the key terms that occur in this section. In column 2, write a definition of each term. Add further key terms that occur throughout the topic.

Now test yourself

Tested

1 What is the energy mix and why is it such an important national issue?

Answer online

Energy is what the world needs to 'fuel' everything, from transport and industry to food supply and heat in our homes. Energy can be derived from a diversity of sources. Today, most comes from fossil fuels and much is consumed in the form of electricity.

Energy security is the extent to which a country can achieve an affordable, reliable and stable energy supply. It is the ability to meet all the national energy needs regardless of any events that might threaten that ability.

Energy mix refers to the different sources of energy that a country uses in meeting its energy needs. It is in the best interests of a country to ensure that its energy mix involves the increasing use of renewable and recyclable energy sources and maximises the use of domestic sources.

Energy supply, demand and security

Energy sources

Revised

Energy sources are commonly grouped as either **non-renewable sources** or **renewable sources** (Table 1.1). It is common to recognise **recyclable sources** as a subgroup within renewable sources, e.g. biomass, biofuels and nuclear power.

Non-renewable sources cannot be replaced once they have been used.

Renewable sources are capable of regeneration on a human timescale.

Recyclable sources have a renewable stock which, with careful management, can be replenished.

Table 1.1 Sources of energy (percentage of global energy supply)

Non-renewable	Renewable	Recyclable
Coal (25%)	Solar (0.5%)	Biomass and biofuels (4%)
Natural gas (23%)	Wind (0.3%)	Nuclear (6%)
Crude oil (37%)	HEP (3%)	
Tar sands and oil shales (<0.1%)	Marine (tidal) (<0.1%)	
Peat and lignite (<0.1%)	Geothermal (0.2%)	

It is a common misconception that **reserves** of coal and natural gas (the known parts of those resources) will become exhausted in the very near future. The rate at which those reserves have been exploited over the last

Examiner's tip

Use this threefold classification of energy sources rather than the twofold distinction between non-renewable and renewable sources.

50 years has been matched by the rate of discovery of new reserves and the more efficient extraction and use of those reserves.

Energy sources are also classified as **primary energy** or **secondary energy**. All the sources in Table 1.1 can provide primary energy, i.e. in the form of heat or physical motion. In reality, most are converted into secondary energy, usually electricity, which is a particularly convenient and easily distributed form of energy.

It is important to understand that these groupings of energy sources have different environmental impacts:

- **Non-renewable sources** (i.e. fossil fuels) produce carbon dioxide during combustion and contribute to global warming and sometimes acid rain from sulphur dioxide emissions.
- **Renewable sources** do not produce carbon dioxide or contribute directly to atmospheric pollution.
- **Recyclable sources** are potentially carbon neutral, which means they produce carbon dioxide when they are used but absorb it when they are grown. Nuclear power does not produce carbon dioxide, but the disposal of nuclear waste poses a major problem.

Revision activity

Learn three examples of each of the three main types of energy source.

Now test yourself   Tested ☐

2   Why is there growing concern about the use of non-renewable sources of energy?
3   Why is nuclear power classified as a recyclable rather than a non-renewable energy source?

Answers online

Typical mistake

Don't confuse traditional biomass fuels such as wood with 'modern' biofuels such as biodiesel and bioethanol.

Typical mistake

Many candidates think that oil is still a major fuel in the generation of electricity, but it has in fact been superceded by gas.

Examiner's tip

Remember that two of the main primary energy sources are coal and natural gas, but that they are also both used to produce secondary energy (electricity).

Examiner's tip

Don't become obsessed with nuclear accidents. Take a balanced view of the costs and benefits of nuclear power.

Access to energy sources   Revised ☐

Access to energy resources varies around the world because:

- the sources of renewable and non-renewable energy are not evenly distributed — some countries are much better endowed than others
- the sources vary in terms of their ease of exploitation — where exploitation is difficult, costs will be high and most likely restrict overall exploitation
- the technology needed to exploit energy sources is not equally available — developed countries are at an advantage here
- the demand for energy and the need to exploit energy sources varies from country to country — in general, the higher the level of economic development, the greater the demand

Revision activity

Make a note of the four factors causing access to energy sources to vary from place to place.

Now test yourself

4   Name four factors that cause access to energy to vary from country to country.
5   Why is technology so important with regard to energy?

Answers online

Tested ☐

Demand for energy

Revised

It is economic development and rising standards of living that lie behind the phenomenal increase in the global demand for energy. Between 2010 and 2030, global demand is expected to grow by nearly 50%.

There are two distinct global distributions — **energy supply** and **energy demand** — and these give rise to three 'energy worlds':

- the **energy-rich countries** where there are vast **surpluses** of supply over demand (e.g. Saudi Arabia)
- the **energy-poor countries** where **energy poverty** means demand far exceeds internal sources of energy (e.g. UK)
- the **energy-neutral countries** where demand and supply are more or less equally balanced (e.g. Brazil)

> **Typical mistake**
>
> When writing about demand, many candidates don't understand the difference between total energy consumption and electricity consumption.

> **Now test yourself**
>
> 6 Why does energy consumption increase with rising living standards?
>
> **Answer online**
>
> Tested

Energy security

Revised

It is in the best interests of all countries to achieve the highest degree of energy security possible. The key to energy security lies in:

- striving for **self-sufficiency** — meeting as much of the energy demand from domestic sources. There are **geopolitical** risks associated with dependence on foreign sources of supply
- achieving a **sustainable energy mix** — using energy derived from a variety of sources (renewable, recyclable and non-renewable), i.e. not being too dependent on just one source
- raising **energy efficiency** — it has been shown that the general demand for energy can be substantially lowered by simple energy-saving measures
- ensuring energy is supplied at an affordable price to industry and consumers

> **Revision activities**
>
> - Learn the energy mix of three contrasting countries, e.g. the UK, France and a developing country such as China.
> - List the four key factors influencing energy security and make brief notes about each.

The impacts of energy insecurity

Energy pathways

Revised

This section is about the possible impacts of a decline in global energy security. This increase in the world's **energy insecurity** results from four main factors (Figure 1.1).

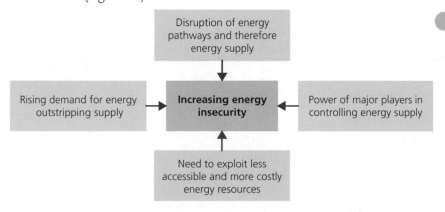

> **Now test yourself**
>
> 7 Outline the main factors giving rise to increasing energy insecurity in the world.
>
> **Answer online**
>
> Tested

Figure 1.1 Increasing energy insecurity

Energy pathways are the vital arteries of the global economy: the wellbeing of many countries depends on them. Many of the major energy pathways fan out from a small number of **energy nodes**, which are major sources of primary energy located in energy-rich countries such as the oilfields of the Middle East and the gas fields of Russia. Most of the pathways end up in energy-poor countries where energy demand far exceeds the supply of energy from internal sources. Pathway destinations include the USA, China, Japan and Europe.

> **Energy pathways** are routes along which energy sources are transported from producer to consumer.

Revision activity

Define 'energy pathways' and 'energy nodes' and note two examples of each.

Examiner's tip

Remember that energy resources are transported in different ways: oil and gas are moved mainly by pipeline and ship, coal mainly by ship and rail, and electricity by cable.

Supply disruption — Revised ☐

The vital flows of energy along the pathways are vulnerable to disruption by:

- the exhaustion of reserves
- **political instability** along the pathways
- **disputes** over the ownership of energy resources or the transmission of energy across national borders by pipeline (e.g. disputes in 2006 and 2009 over payment and prices led to Russia cutting off gas supplies to Ukraine, thereby reducing supplies down-line to France and Germany)
- **terrorism** and possible attacks on energy infrastructure
- **sudden price rises** for imported energy
- **natural hazards** such as earthquakes, tsunamis and hurricanes (Hurricane Katrina in 2005 did extensive damage to oil refineries)

The risks of disruption are greatest at narrow **choke points**, such as the Straits of Hormuz at the entrance to the Persian Gulf and through which passes some 30% of the world's crude oil supply. The impacts of supply disruption include:

- rises in the cost of energy, as during the 1973 Oil Crisis
- the need to search for alternative energy sources with more secure pathways
- reduced economic output and employment during periods of disruption
- social unrest related to rising energy costs and unemployment

Heavy dependence on a small number of pathways can greatly increase the potential impacts of disruption.

Revision activities

- List five scenarios that could result in the disruption of energy pathways.
- On a world map, plot the top ten oil producers and the top ten oil consumers. Refer to the BP Statistical Review 2012 at www.bp.com/statisticalreview.
- Research the gas pipeline dispute between Russia and Ukraine and draw a timeline of events.

Now test yourself

8 Identify some of the consequences of the disruption of energy supplies.

9 What are energy nodes and energy pathway choke points?

Answers online

Tested ☐

The search for new sources — Revised ☐

The search for new sources of energy is driven by two needs:

- to meet the ever-increasing global demand for energy
- to make countries more energy secure, i.e. less dependent on imported supplies and less at risk if these are disrupted

The search is moving in two main directions:

- looking for new reserves of non-renewable energy, particularly oil and gas

- developing new sources of energy, particularly those that are renewable, such as wind, solar and wind power

For non-renewable energy, the most accessible reserves have already been found and exploited. The search for new resources focuses on the discovery in more **technically difficult areas** such as within the Arctic circle and deep sea. Oil is being extracted from relatively new sources such as oil shales and tar sands. **Fracking** (rock cracking) is being used to extract natural gas, a method that has already become a major source of gas in the USA. These developments have all been made possible and viable by recent advances in technology.

There is great concern about the environmental impacts of this continuing search for new reserves, as well as the exploitation of these new sources of oil and gas. Oil spills can cause immense damage, particularly in **environmentally sensitive areas**.

Revision activity

Note the two main directions in which the search for new sources of fossil fuel energy is moving and the challenges associated with both.

Now test yourself   Tested

10 What drives the search for new sources of energy?

Answer online

Energy players   Revised

The six major **players** in the global supply of energy are shown in Figure 1.2. Of these major players, two are particularly powerful:

- the very large **TNCs** (e.g. Exxon Mobil, Royal Dutch Shell and BP) and the state-owned oil and gas companies (e.g. Saudi Aramco of Saudi Arabia, CNPC of China and Gazprom of Russia). Both are involved in the exploration, extraction, refining and delivery of oil and gas
- **OPEC** (Organization of the Petroleum Exporting Countries) and **GECF** (Gas Exporting Countries Forum), whose member countries are responsible for a large percentage of global oil and gas production. They are able to control the amount that is produced at any one time and as a result determine the price of these two energy sources

Players are individuals, groups or organisations with a stake in a particular issue and the ability to influence outcomes.

Pressure groups include conservation and environmental organisations such as WWF and Greenpeace.

Intergovernmental organisations include those that are particularly concerned with the trade in energy, such as the World Bank and the World Trade Organization.

Consumers include households, industrial activities and public utilities.

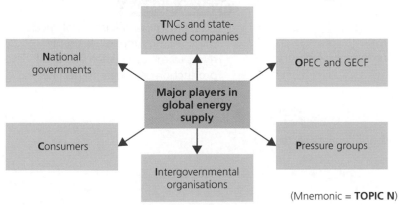

(Mnemonic = **TOPIC N**)

Figure 1.2 Major players in the supply of global energy

Energy security and the future

Key concepts ——————————————————————————————— Revised ☐

There are many questions to be asked about the future global energy
situation. Will the demand for energy continue to rise indefinitely? Will
it be possible to supply that rising demand? How energy secure will the
world become?

Uncertainties over global energy supply ———————————— Revised ☐

The main uncertainties concerning future energy security are shown in
Figure 1.3. Of these, the most significant is the rate at which the global
demand for energy will continue to rise, which will be determined by a
range of factors including the:

● rate of population growth

● rate of global economic growth and rising living standards

● rate of economic development in developing countries and the BRICs

● degree to which the energy demands of the energy-poor least-
developed world are met

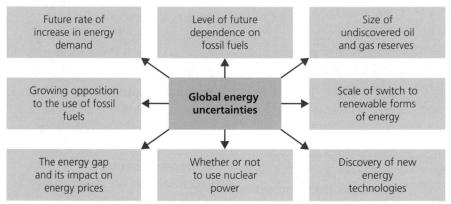

Figure 1.3 Global energy uncertainties

Typical mistake

The term '**peak oil**' does not mean
there will no more oil. It simply
refers to the time when global oil
production will begin to decline.

Responses to increasing demands

There are various responses to increasing demands for energy, including:

- continuing to use **fossil fuels** and exploring for new reserves and sources of oil and gas
- switching to **renewable sources** of energy such as biofuels, wind, solar, HEP, tidal and geothermal power
- making greater use of **nuclear power**
- taking steps to increase the **efficiency** with which we use energy, thereby reducing current energy demands, i.e. **energy conservation**

What needs to be stressed is that there is no 'silver bullet' solution: none of the above choices receives universal approval. There are profound differences of opinion, particularly concerning **costs** and **benefits**. However, the common objective should be to achieve a sustainable energy mix.

> **Typical mistake**
>
> The Kyoto Protocol is about the reduction of carbon dioxide emissions. It is not specifically about switching to renewable energy sources.

> **Revision activity**
>
> Create a table of the costs and benefits of developing different renewable and recyclable energy sources. Use sub-headings in your table (social, political, economic and environmental).

> **Now test yourself**   Tested
>
> 13 What are the main factors influencing the rate at which global energy demand increases?
>
> 14 Give some examples of different ways in which energy can be used more efficiently.
>
> **Answers online**

Geopolitical tensions and conflict

Geopolitical tensions and possible conflicts may occur over energy sources because of:

- the mismatch between the distributions of energy demand and energy supply. This means that energy-poor countries are forced to import energy from other countries and that energy-rich countries are in a position to hold those energy-poor countries to ransom
- the degree to which large and powerful nations are gaining hold of the energy resources in less-developed parts of the world — China's move into Africa is one such example
- the promotion of biofuels is taking over large areas of land that once grew food. In turn, this is leading to higher food prices and, in some countries, to food shortages, malnutrition and food riots

The bottom line here is that all countries should strive to become as energy self-sufficient as possible.

> **Geopolitical** relates to the relationships between a country and the rest of the world in such areas as sovereignty, economic cooperation, trade, defence and decision-making.

> **Revision activities**
>
> - In your own words, write a definition of the term 'geopolitical'.
> - Note three examples of energy-rich countries and three energy-poor countries.

> **Now test yourself**   Tested
>
> 15 What is meant by 'China's move into Africa' and why is it happening?
>
> **Answer online**

Meeting future energy needs

Meeting future energy needs and raising the level of energy security means that we must take some brave decisions and some bold actions. It is widely agreed that our future energy strategy cannot be one of **'business as usual'** with its unsustainable dependence on polluting fossil fuels. The best way forward lies in combining a number of specific energy options. These possible options might be labelled 'the five energy Rs':

- **Reduce** overall energy consumption — focus on ways of raising energy efficiency in the home, industry and transport and abandon wasteful ways, e.g. replace petrol and diesel engines with ones driven by hydrogen or electricity produced from renewable sources.

- **Reject** environmentally damaging and polluting energy sources — if total rejection is not possible, seek to minimise the environmental damage associated with both their extraction and their use (i.e. carbon emissions) by introducing tight controls.

- **Research** and develop more sustainable and affordable sources of energy, i.e. renewable sources such as wind, solar and tidal power, HEP and biofuels.

- **Recycle** waste and convert it into energy, e.g. make use of the methane created in landfill sites.

- **Reaffirm** that nuclear power is vital in bridging the **energy gap** between demand and supply, at least in the short to medium term.

Examiner's tip

Physical factors, particularly climate and relief, restrict the availability and potential use of renewable sources of energy in many parts of the world. The impact of NIMBY-ism tends to be overstated.

Revision activity

Learn the 'five energy Rs' (reduce, reject, research, recycle and reaffirm) and make sure you know what each involves.

Now test yourself

16 Why is a 'business as usual' energy strategy a non-starter?

17 Why is the nuclear option such a controversial one?

18 What is the link between the energy gap and the price of energy?

Answers online

Exam practice

Section A questions

1 The diagram below shows the relative potential of different sources of renewable energy.

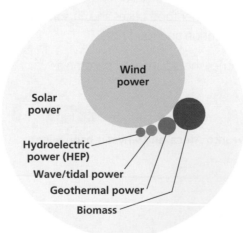

(a) Explain the differences in the potential of these renewable energy sources. [10]

(b) Assess the role that fossil fuels might play in future energy security. [15]

Answers and quick quizzes at **www.therevisionbutton.co.uk/myrevisionnotes**

2 The diagram below gives four predictions for global energy.

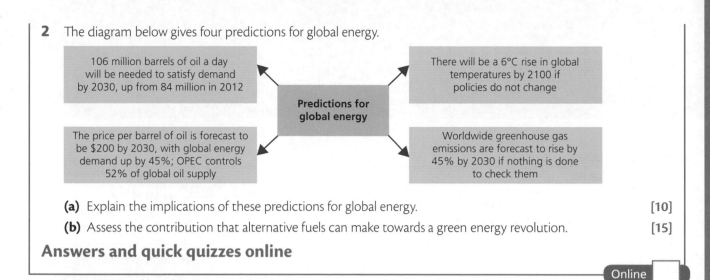

106 million barrels of oil a day will be needed to satisfy demand by 2030, up from 84 million in 2012

Predictions for global energy

There will be a 6°C rise in global temperatures by 2100 if policies do not change

The price per barrel of oil is forecast to be $200 by 2030, with global energy demand up by 45%; OPEC controls 52% of global oil supply

Worldwide greenhouse gas emissions are forecast to rise by 45% by 2030 if nothing is done to check them

(a) Explain the implications of these predictions for global energy. **[10]**

(b) Assess the contribution that alternative fuels can make towards a green energy revolution. **[15]**

Answers and quick quizzes online

Online

Examiner's summary

✔ Energy sources can be split into renewable, non-renewable and recyclable. Concern about the use of these energy sources centres on the non-renewables for two reasons: once used, they cannot be replaced and they are fossil fuels which, when used, create atmospheric pollution and contribute to global warming.

✔ There are two critical energy distributions: one of energy supply and another of energy demand. The mismatch between the two distributions leads to the creation of three types of energy situation: energy surplus or energy-rich where supply exceeds demand; energy deficit or energy-poor where demand exceeds supply; energy-neutral where supply and demand are more or less equal.

✔ It is in the best interests of all countries to achieve energy security. This may be achieved in three ways: by becoming as self-sufficient as possible, i.e. by not relying on imported supplies; by achieving a sustainable mix of energy resources; by raising the efficiency with which energy is used.

✔ Critical in the world of energy are the pathways that link the locations of energy supply with the locations of energy demand. Disruption of these pathways and sources of energy supply can have serious consequences.

✔ One way of avoiding the risks of disruption is to explore new sources of energy in areas that are deemed to be safer and that are nearer to the locations of energy demand. Exploration requires large inputs of technology and capital.

✔ The global supply of energy is in the hands of some very powerful players who are capable of holding many countries to ransom, especially energy-poor countries.

✔ Achieving energy security is handicapped by a number of uncertainties, perhaps the most critical of which is forecasting the rate at which the global demand for energy will increase.

✔ The mismatch between the distributions of energy supply and demand is creating geopolitical tensions that could easily lead to conflicts.

✔ The risk that energy demand will outstrip supply makes it all the more critical that we observe the 'five energy Rs' as they define the pathway to a more sustainable and energy secure future.

2 Water conflicts

Key concepts

Revised

Water, like energy, is a fundamental human need, being required for such basic purposes as drinking, washing, sewage disposal, agriculture and industry.

Water conflict, present and predicted, arises from three circumstances:

- the widening global **water gap** produced by the rising demand for water and the static or diminishing supply of water
- the existence of water-surplus and water-deficit areas
- the competition between different and often incompatible users for the same water resources

The last two conflicts can exist both between countries and within them.

Revision activity

Create a two-column table. In column 1, list the key terms that occur in this section. In column 2, write a definition of each term. Add further key terms that occur throughout the topic.

Now test yourself

1 What is the water gap and what are the main factors causing it?

Answer online

Tested

The geography of water supply

Water supply

Revised

Because the Earth is a closed system, water is a **finite resource**, which makes it a fundamental issue for water supply. The oceans hold 97.5% of the global water store, but this is salt water and undrinkable. Only 2.5% is freshwater and most of this is locked up in ice, snow and permafrost.

The global distribution of water is controlled by three main factors:

- **Climate** — this is the most significant in that the global distribution of water reflects the Earth's climatic zones with their distinctive rainfall regimes. Rainfall frequently varies with the seasons.
- **Geology** — permeable rock allows rainfall to pass into underground drainage systems; **aquifers** such as chalk and porous sandstone can store vast quantities of water underground. Impermeable rock ensures that rainfall is relatively quickly fed into surface river systems.
- **Surface processes such as river systems** — river basins collect and store huge quantities of water and rivers transfer much of that water from one place to another.

Note that water scarcity is not highest at the equator. It is greatest in the arid areas that straddle the Tropics or occur in continental interiors.

Examiner's tip

Remember how little of the Earth's water is freshwater available for human consumption.

An **aquifer** is an underground store of groundwater in porous rock. Water is extracted from these subterranean stores mainly by wells and boreholes.

Typical mistake

Candidates often lack an understanding of what groundwater is and how it is extracted.

Revision activity

List the three main factors controlling the global distribution of water and make brief notes about each.

Now test yourself

2 Why is there so little global water available for human use?
3 What do you think will be the impact of global warming and climate change on global water supplies?

Answers online

Tested

The mismatch between water supply and demand

Revised

The relentless rise in the global demand for water is caused by:

- **increasing population** — more people, so more thirsts to quench
- **economic development** — greater use of water in farming and industry
- **rising living standards** — more water wanted in the home for washing, cleaning and the treatment of waste

Just as the availability of water (i.e. water supply) varies from place to place, so too does the demand for water. This mismatch creates areas of **water deficit** and **water surplus**. Two degrees of water deficit are recognised:

- **water stress** occurs where water supply is less than 1700 m³ per person per year
- **water scarcity** occurs where water supply falls below 1000 m³ per person per year (Figure 2.1)

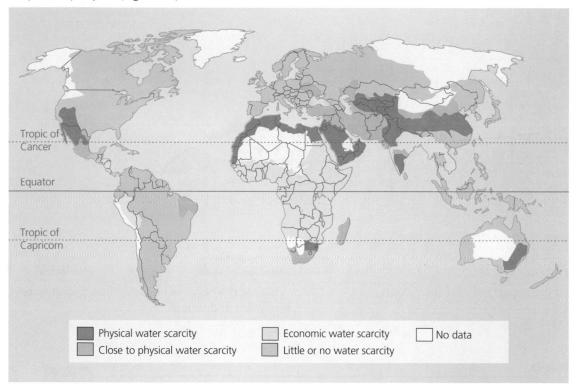

Figure 2.1 Water scarcity

There are two types of water scarcity:

- **physical**, which occurs when 75% of a country's or area's water resources are being used
- **economic**, which occurs when the development of water resources is limited by a lack of capital and technology, and water is expensive

Examiner's tip

Meeting the rising demand for water is a particular challenge facing the emergent economies, especially **China** and **India**.

Now test yourself

Tested

4   What are the main reasons for the rising global demand for water?

Answer online

Revision activity

List the three main reasons for the rise in global demand for water.

Human activity

Revised

People are having two major negative impacts on water availability and supply:

- On quantity by **over-abstraction** of water — once this has taken place, it is difficult to fully recharge rivers and underground stores. Over-abstraction of groundwater can have a number of unwanted consequences such as land subsidence, salinisation of wells and boreholes, and loss of ecologically valuable wetlands.
- On quality by **pollution** of rivers and groundwater — this results from actions such as the discharge of sewage and industrial waste in rivers, the seepage of chemical fertilisers into groundwater stores and the accumulation of sediments behind dams.

These impacts have serious knock-on effects, i.e. increases in both water stress and **water insecurity**. Figure 2.2 shows seven human impacts on water supply and quality.

> **Water insecurity** means not having access to sufficient supplies of safe (clean) water.
>
> **Over-abstraction** is the extraction and consumption of surface and groundwater resources beyond their sustainable level, so that the resource gradually becomes depleted.
>
> **Pollution** is the release of harmful substances into the environment with the potential to harm both people and the natural environment.

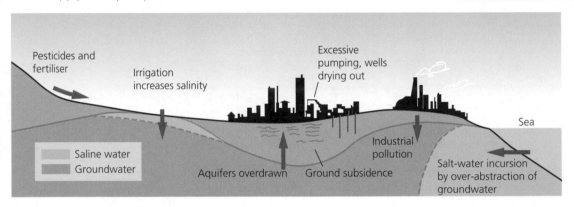

Figure 2.2 Human impacts on water supply and quality

Revision activity

Make notes about the impacts of over-abstraction and pollution on water supplies.

Now test yourself

Tested

5   What are the negative impacts of people on water availability and supply?

Answer online

Access to water

Revised

It is estimated that there are over 1 billion people in today's world who do not have access to an adequate supply of **safe water**. They suffer from **water poverty**. The degree of water poverty is assessed by looking at five aspects of water management:

- **use** — how efficiently water is used in the home, and by agriculture and industry
- **resources** — the quantity of available water
- **access** — time and distance involved in obtaining safe water
- **capacity** — how well water supply is managed
- **environment** — water quality and sustainability of supply

Many of the people suffering from water poverty live in parts of the world where there is physical water scarcity (Figure 2.1). However, water poverty also coincides with the incidence of financial and economic poverty. This suggests a link between economic water scarcity and poverty.

> **Safe water** is water that is sufficiently clean to be fit for human use and consumption.

Examiner's tip

There are two types of water poverty: physical, when there is simply no available water, and economic, when people do not have the capital or technology to supply the water they need.

Lack of water prevents the reduction of poverty and restricts development. Improved water supply can increase food production and, along with improved sanitation, bring better health and wellbeing. Water wealth is an important factor in the prosperity of more developed countries.

Now test yourself   Tested ☐

6   Why is it important to distinguish between available water and safe water?
7   What are the benefits of an improved water supply?
8   Is water poverty necessarily confined to areas of physical water scarcity? Give reasons to support your answer.

Answers online

The risks of water insecurity

Water supply problems   Revised ☐

The world is moving into a future of increasing water insecurity. This will threaten not only economic development, human health and wellbeing, but also international relations. Water insecurity is considered a much greater threat than energy insecurity (see Topic 1), if only because there is no substitute for water.

A secure water supply is essential to both economic development and human wellbeing. Attaining it can be prevented by a range of obstacles, including:

● **inadequate water resources** because of a low-rainfall climate and few rivers
● **seasonality** in both climate and river flow
● **lack of infrastructure** needed to produce safe water
● **competition** between water users such as agriculture, fishing, industry, transport and households
● **environmental impacts** of over-abstraction, particularly the reduction of groundwater sources
● **mismatch** between areas of demand and areas of supply
● **water pollution**

Examiner's tip

In this and other topics you should learn some case studies, but use the information from them selectively and as part of a wider discussion. To simply repeat one of your case studies will not answer the question in front of you.

Revision activity

List the seven obstacles to achieving a secure water supply and make brief notes about each of them.

Now test yourself

9   Explain what is meant by the term 'water insecurity'.
10 Why is seasonality a potential water supply problem?

Answers online
                                                            Tested ☐

Water conflicts   Revised ☐

When the demand for water overtakes supply and several **stakeholders** wish to use the same resource, there is potential for conflict. Part of the ongoing tension in the Middle East between Israel, Palestine, Jordan, Syria and Lebanon is explained by the fact that all these countries rely heavily for their water supply on the same two sources: the River Jordan and its lakes and three important aquifers.

Stakeholders are essentially the same as **players**, i.e. individuals, groups or organisations that have an interest in the development or outcomes of a particular project.

Typical mistake

The term 'conflict' as used in this and other topics rarely refers to war. Rather, it is used in the sense of a contest or clash between different uses and users or between different ideas and values.

Potential conflicts over water can arise in a number of different circumstances, for example:

● where two countries share the same river — it might be where the river serves as a frontier (e.g. the River Paraná between Argentina, Brazil and Uruguay) or where the river flows from one country to another (e.g. the Ganges from India to Bangladesh). The second situation means that the upstream country is in a position to control the river waters at the expense of the country that is located downstream

● where there are competing and incompatible demands on water supply, particularly within a country, from activities such as fishing, irrigation, power generation, industry, domestic use and recreation (e.g. the Aral Sea)

● where there is confrontation between development of the resources of a river or lake and a strong case for conservation of the natural environment

The locations of these potential conflicts are sometimes referred to as **water pressure points**. Figure 2.3 shows that they arise from three overlapping circumstances. As the demand for water outstrips supply or as water availability diminishes, water conflicts are likely to become more frequent and possibly more intense.

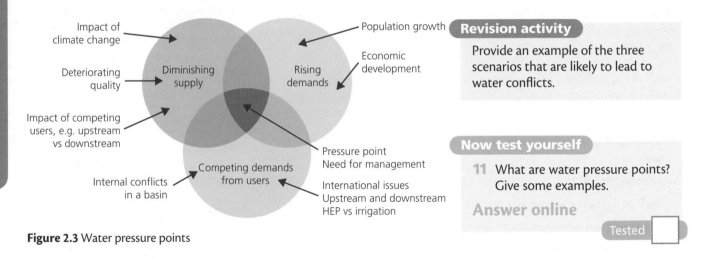

Figure 2.3 Water pressure points

Revision activity

Provide an example of the three scenarios that are likely to lead to water conflicts.

Now test yourself

11 What are water pressure points? Give some examples.

Answer online

Tested ☐

Water geopolitics

Revised ☐

So far as water is concerned, geopolitics is mainly about international conflicts, treaties and agreements. In general, the player with the greatest military, economic and political power is most likely to be the winner in any conflict. This means that international agreements are vital if conflicts and tensions are to be avoided. The main players in global water matters are discussed in the next section (page 22).

Equitable use is a concept that all countries involved in water-sharing situations should recognise and observe. It means ensuring that all interested parties have a fair share of the water resources. The criteria used for deciding this sharing include:

● the amount of available water

● the degree of dependency on the shared water source

● the scale of **water need**

Answers and quick quizzes at **www.therevisionbutton.co.uk/myrevisionnotes**

- **downstream impacts** of abstraction and use
- **prior use** (a problematic one in that it constrains the scale of possible future use)

There are 'rules' for sharing water resources equitably called the Helsinki Rules (1966) and the updated Berlin Rules (2004), but they are not always applied.

Revision activities

- Make notes about the equitable use of water, particularly the five criteria that are used.
- Find out more about the Helsinki Rules that apply to the use of international rivers and the Berlin Rules on water resources.

Now test yourself — Tested

12 What is meant by the term 'equitable use' and why is it an important concept?

Answer online

Water pathways — Revised

A particular feature of water supply is the transfer of great quantities of water, often over considerable distances. This is necessary where there is a mismatch between the distributions of water availability and water demand. Water surpluses have to be transferred to those areas where the level of water demand creates water deficits. The pipelines and canals used in this transfer of water are **water pathways**.

Examples of large-scale **water transfer schemes** include the Tagus-Segura scheme in Spain, the Snowy Mountains scheme in southeast Australia and the immense South to North project in China which is now under construction. Because they require much investment and engineering, such transfer schemes are only undertaken if there are considerable net benefits. However, costs may be incurred in both the source and receiving areas, as well as in-between. These costs include:

- the adverse environmental impacts of the water transfer infrastructure, e.g. the construction of dams and reservoirs, pumping stations, pipelines and canals
- the possibility of water scarcity in the source area due to the loss of available water
- a greater and more wasteful use of water because of the increased availability of water in the receiving area, e.g. more irrigation, more golf courses, more water sports facilities
- pipelines being vulnerable to sabotage and terrorist attacks

Revision activity

List some large-scale water transfer schemes.

Now test yourself

13 What are the risks associated with water transfer schemes?

Answer online — Tested

Water conflicts and the future

The nature of the world's water future and the likelihood of water conflicts will depend on four main factors:

- the rate at which the global water demand increases
- the degree to which those demands can be met by supplies
- the development of water management strategies to maximise the use of available water
- the development of water technologies to harness new sources of water

Revision activity

Make a note of the four factors that will determine the avoidance of future water conflicts.

Trends in water demand

It is clear that the global demand for water will continue to rise, due mainly to:

- **increasing population**
- **economic development** and the continuing growth of the global economy
- **rising living standards**

Most critical here is the rate of increase. Forecasts indicate that agriculture will continue to be the dominant water consumer, accounting for about two-thirds of demand, with industry and domestic use accounting equally for the remaining one-third.

Examiner's tip

The rate of increase in water demand is likely to be high in developing countries as they industrialise and become more urbanised. In developed countries, water demand is less likely to increase much.

Now test yourself

Tested

14 What are the three main factors affecting the rise in the global demand for water?

Answer online

Responses to rising demands

The huge challenge of meeting future water demands and ensuring water security lies in the hands of a range of **players**, such as:

- **water companies** — their responsibilities include providing a supply of safe water in a cost-effective and efficient way
- **governments** — it is for them to decide which water sources to rely on and how best to achieve a high degree of water security
- **international organisations** — these must ensure that the principle of equitable use is observed and that everyone has access to safe water (World Bank, UNESCO)
- **consumers** — farmers, industrialists and householders must seek to constrain their use of water and maximise the efficiency with which they use it
- **environmentalists** — these have more of a watchdog role to ensure that the supply of water is sustainable and not inflicting irreparable environmental damage

Revision activity

List the main players that are responsible for ensuring that rising water demands are met.

Now test yourself

15 Which uses are the three main consumers of water?

Answer online

Tested

Water management strategies

Managing future water supplies requires actions at a variety of levels. These should range from large-scale projects funded by governments and international agencies, such as the World Bank, down to the local level of changing individual consumers' attitudes to water use and their consequent actions.

Large-scale water management projects involve **hard engineering** and include:

- the **collection of surface freshwater** by means of mega-dams and storing it in reservoirs — at present, two-thirds of all surface freshwater is abstracted in this way

- long-distance **water transfer schemes**, such as those that are now under way in China, Brazil and Spain
- **desalinisation**, which is a relative newcomer, but much is now being done in water-stressed but technologically advanced countries such as the Middle Eastern states, Japan and the USA
- **restoring wetlands** so that they can once again act as vital water stores, as in the northern part of the Aral Sea

Water management at a local level is more about **conservation**. Bottom-up actions include:

- making crop irrigation much more efficient — replacing wasteful sprinklers and surface flood irrigation with advanced drip irrigation schemes
- reusing industrial and domestic grey water
- installing a water meter in every home, which will hopefully encourage more careful water use
- harvesting roof rain and collecting it in butts
- reducing leakage from local water supply networks
- ensuring that wells and boreholes are not over-pumped

It is widely agreed that **integrated water management** is needed to deal with the threat of water scarcity. This involves a focus on the management of groundwater sources, waterways and water use in urban areas, together with the use of technology to constantly monitor performance in these three areas of management.

> **Desalinisation** is the removal of salt from sea water to make it fit for human use and consumption.

Revision activities

- Make notes about what is involved in a hard engineering approach to water management.
- List the six actions that might be taken at a local level to conserve water resources.

Now test yourself

16 What are the main environmental costs of mega-dams and large-scale water transfer schemes?

17 Why is the management of urban water an important part of integrated water management?

Answers online

Tested ☐

The role of technology

Revised ☐

Technology is already playing an important part in helping to raise the supply of water, with examples including the hard-engineering projects given above.

- On the supply side, the use of technology involves finding ways of making desalinisation less costly and more available to developing countries and reducing the environmental impacts of water abstraction and transfer.
- On the demand side, the use of technology is centred on finding ways of using water more efficiently, thereby reducing consumption.

What is certain is that human resourcefulness and technology are going to face an even greater challenge in an era of climate change.

Examiner's tip

Remember that the equipment used for desalinisation is both expensive and a heavy consumer of energy.

Examiner's tip

There are two routes to increasing water supply in developing countries: by local initiatives using intermediate technology and by large-scale civil engineering projects backed by foreign funding and technical support.

Now test yourself

Tested ☐

18 How might technology help on the demand side of the water equation?

Answer online

Exam practice

Section A questions

1 The diagram below shows the widening water gap.

(a) Using the diagram and your own knowledge, explain why the gap between the water 'haves' and the 'have-nots' is likely to widen in the next 20 years.　　　　　　　　　　　　　　**[10]**

(b) Evaluate the roles that different types of technology can play in improving water security.　　**[15]**

2 The figure below gives solutions to the global water crisis.

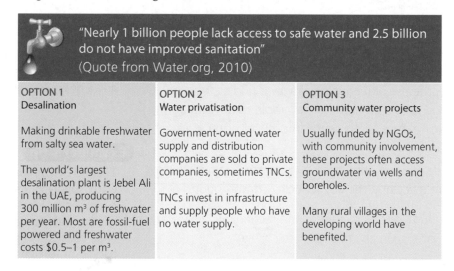

(a) Explain the contribution that the three options might make towards solving the global water crisis.　　**[10]**

(b) Using examples, assess how climate change and economic growth might contribute to a future global water crisis.　　**[15]**

Answers and quick quizzes online

Examiner's summary

✔ Water is vital to human survival and is needed for a range of different activities. It plays a crucial role in economic development and is an important component of our quality of life.

✔ Only a small percentage of global water is freshwater and suitable for most human uses. The amount of global freshwater is finite and the demands being placed on it are increasing all the time.

✔ There is a widespread mismatch between the distributions of water availability (supply) and water demand. This mismatch is responsible for the creation of areas of water stress and water scarcity.

✔ People have negative impacts on both the quantity and quality of water. Access to water is often related to and controlled by wealth and poverty.

✔ Water insecurity poses a threat to economic development and human wellbeing. Ensuring a secure and reliable water supply is a top priority for many countries, but achieving it is beset by a range of physical and human obstacles.

✔ There is a prospect of increasing international tensions and possible conflicts arising from the drive of individual countries to achieve a secure supply of water for themselves. Water pressure points are likely to occur where a major river is shared by two or more countries. The principle of equitable use must be applied and recognised by all interested parties.

✔ The pathways or pipelines that carry water from water-surplus to water-deficit areas deliver immense benefits, particularly where there is a high water demand. However, there are also considerable costs of a largely environmental kind. They are also strategically vulnerable.

✔ It seems highly likely that the demand for water will continue to increase. To meet this demand requires actions to be taken on both the demand and supply sides as part of integrated water management programmes. A top-down hard engineering approach to water management has an important part to play here, so too a whole series of bottom-up conservation actions.

3 Biodiversity under threat

Key concepts

Biodiversity is a key resource that provides a range of valuable **goods** and **services**. It is the product of natural processes and for this reason varies throughout the world. Biodiversity is under threat because its goods and services are being over-exploited. Some also claim that it is being threatened by climate change.

Wellbeing is a generic term for a group of overlapping concepts, which include quality of life, satisfaction and welfare. Some more specific constituents of wellbeing include:

- **security** — personal safety; access to water, food and energy; protection from disasters
- **life materials** — adequate ways of making a living; sufficient food and water; shelter
- **health** — access to clean air and water; feeling well; strength
- **social relations** — mutual respect; a sense of belonging; the ability to help others

It is increasingly recognised that human wellbeing is closely linked with ecological wellbeing (i.e. biodiversity).

Revision activity

Create a two-column table. In column 1, list the key terms that occur in this section. In column 2, write a definition of each term. Add further key terms that occur throughout the topic.

Defining biodiversity

Defining biodiversity

Biodiversity is the total sum of genes, species and ecosystems in a given area: the greater the number, the greater the diversity.

Genetic diversity is the range of genes found within a particular species. The degree of resistance to pests and diseases is often determined by the degree of diversity. **Species diversity** is the range or variety of plant and animal species present in an ecosystem. Species diversity helps an ecosystem to withstand and adjust to changing physical conditions. **Ecosystem diversity** is the number of different ecosystems in an area. This diversity is largely determined by physical conditions (e.g. climate, geology, relief and soils).

Answers and quick quizzes at **www.therevisionbutton.co.uk/myrevisionnotes**

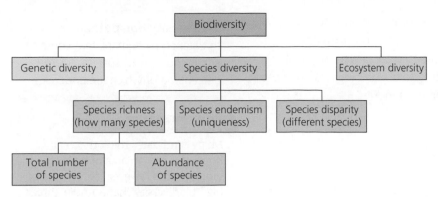

Figure 3.1 What is biodiversity?

Figure 3.1 makes the important point that any assessment of biodiversity should take into account the diversity of each of these three components. Note that there are three significantly different aspects to species diversity:

- **species richness** — the number of species and the abundance of individual species
- **species endemism** — the degree to which individual species are confined to a particular area
- **species disparity** — the differences between species

The most biodiverse places left in today's world tend to be highlands and islands — in other words, places that are remote from human settlement and exploitation.

Factors that influence biodiversity

Revised

At a global scale, the factors that have most impact on biodiversity are **physical factors** and include:

- size of area
- climate (temperature, precipitation and amount of light)
- rate of nutrient recycling
- topography and altitude
- degree of isolation
- climate change

More locally the same physical factors apply, but include others such as natural disasters. However, **human factors** can also have a great impact, such as:

- hunting, fishing and the exploitation of other goods and services
- introduction of exotic or alien species
- clearance for agriculture and settlement

However, human factors are not all negative in their impacts. For example, conservation can do much to restore losses in biodiversity caused by human actions.

Hotspots

Revised

At a global level, biodiversity strongly correlates with latitude and climate, with the highest levels occurring within the tropics. In general, biodiversity declines with increasing latitude. Within those latitudinal bands, especially within the tropics, there are variations that give rise to **biodiversity hotspots**. As shown in Figure 3.2, 25 land-based areas were originally identified as biodiversity hotspots, with an additional 9 regions since being added. These hotspots fall into one of three categories:

- continental hotspots, e.g. Brazil's Cerrado
- large island hotspots, e.g. Madagascar
- small island hotspots, e.g. Sri Lanka

In addition, 11 marine hotspots are also recognised. All of them contain coral reefs and are especially threatened by human activities. They account for only 0.02% of the oceans.

Biodiversity hotspots are areas threatened by humans that contain a large number of species, a large percentage of which are endemics.

Typical mistake

Many candidates think that a hotspot is just an area of high biodiversity. However, it is an area of high biodiversity that is under threat.

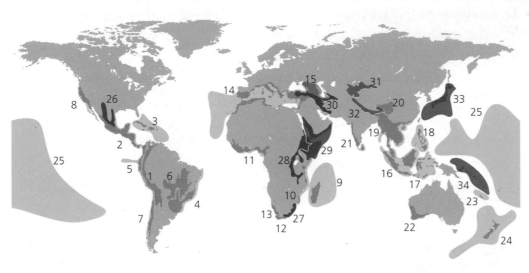

Original hotspots
1 The Tropical Andes
2 Mesoamerica
3 The Caribbean Islands
4 The Atlantic Forest
5 Tumbes-Chocó-Magdalena
6 The Cerrado
7 Chilean Winter Rainfall-Valdivian Forests
8 The California Floristic Province
9 Madagascar and the Indian Ocean Islands
10 The Coastal Forests of Eastern Africa
11 The Guinean Forests of West Africa
12 The Cape Floristic Region
13 The Succulent Karoo

14 The Mediterranean Basin
15 The Caucasus
16 Sundaland
17 Wallacea
18 The Philippines
19 Indo-Burma
20 The Mountains of Southwest China
21 Western Ghats and Sri Lanka
22 Southwest Australia
23 New Caledonia
24 New Zealand
25 Polynesia and Micronesia

Additional hostspots
26 The Madrean Pine-Oak Woodlands
27 Maputaland-Pondoland-Albany
28 The Eastern Afromontane
29 The Horn of Africa
30 The Irano-Anatolian
31 The Mountains of Central Asia
32 Eastern Himalaya
33 Japan
34 East Melanesian Islands

Figure 3.2 Global distribution of land-based biodiversity hotspots

Revision activities

- Write a definition of the term 'biodiversity hotspot'.
- List the three types of hotspot and give examples of each.

Examiner's tip

Learn the names and locations of at least one of each of the three types of land-based biodiversity hotspot.

Now test yourself   Tested ☐

3 What are biodiversity hotspots?
4 Why does biodiversity decrease with latitude?
5 What do most of the 11 marine hotspots have in common?

Answers online

The value of ecosystems

Revised

People obtain a range of benefits from ecosystems, which are usually referred to as goods (or provisioning services) and services. Examples of each include:

- **goods** — food, water, timber, fibre and fuel
- **services** — these are of two types:
  - regulating: climate stability, floods and disease prevention, as well as water purification
  - cultural: recreational, educational, aesthetic and spiritual value

Important links can be identified between these goods and services and different aspects of human wellbeing. For example:

- the goods that are available can contribute a great deal to security and life materials
- regulating services, such as water purification, can have a beneficial impact on health
- cultural services are likely to affect both health and social relations

The actual goods and services provided vary according to the physical and biological characteristics of each ecosystem. Equally important is the fact that different **players** or ecosystem users attach different values to the goods and services. These different evaluations can lead easily to conflicts over the use of goods and services.

Biodiversity threats

Distribution of threatened areas

Revised

A number of methods are used to assess biodiversity threats and their distributions. As the methodologies are different, it is hardly surprising that they come up with slightly different results:

- **Ecosystem Scorecard** — identifies freshwater ecosystems as the most eco-stressed.
- **Living Planet Index** — identifies that freshwater ecosystems are seriously threatened, as well as forest, grassland and marine ecosystems.
- **IUCN Red List** — an annual listing of endangered species that allows for the identification of extinction hotspots. These are located for the most part in the tropical rainforests, tropical grasslands, polar areas and small islands. Freshwater ecosystems are again identified as having a high percentage of threatened species.
- **Millennium Ecosystem Assessment** — highlights the tropical grasslands, marine and freshwater ecosystems and rainforests as under the greatest threat.

There are two distinct distributions: threatened hotspots and areas with threatened species. All methodologies put the spotlight on freshwater ecosystems. Here, the main threat is the widespread and large-scale reclamation of wetlands to provide land for agriculture, industry and urban growth.

Global factors

The threats to global biodiversity come from a number of different directions, including:

- climate change, which is particularly the case if it occurs at such a rapid rate that many species are unable to adapt
- rising sea levels, which threaten to drown large areas and their ecosystems
- unsustainably high rates of population growth and resource consumption
- economic systems promoted by governments and large businesses that fail to value the environment and its resources
- global-scale pollution such as acid rain
- deforestation
- desertification, which is the outcome of both climate change and population pressure
- disease
- ignorance about the need to manage and conserve biodiversity

> **Examiner's tip**
>
> Rising sea levels are one threat posed by global warming. Another is that it will alter and disrupt latitudinal zones, mainly by pushing them towards the poles.

Revision activities

- Draw a spider diagram showing the factors which threaten biodiversity.
- Research and make notes about the threats to either coral reefs or tropical rainforests.

Now test yourself

Tested

8 What are the most threatened ecosystems and what is it that particularly threatens them?
9 Are the causes of desertification physical or human?

Answers online

Ecosystem processes

There are two processes fundamental to the functioning of an ecosystem:

- **Energy flows** — these are movements of energy through an ecosystem, starting with the conversion of sunlight into energy by photosynthesis. Energy then passes up through trophic levels, but energy is lost at each level as a result of respiration and biomass decay.
- **Nutrient cycling** — this is the circulation of chemical elements and compounds from the environment to organisms and then back to the environment. Nutrients are stored in three parts of the ecosystem: soil, living biomass and surface litter. These stores are linked by three pathways: a growth or uptake pathway involves plants taking nutrients from the soil; a fallout pathway leads from biomass to surface litter; a decay pathway leads to the breakdown of litter into humus in the soil.

> **Revision activity**
>
> Draw an annotated diagram to show the nutrient flows between the three stores: soil, biomass and litter.

Both these processes are easily disturbed by a whole range of human actions, from farming to forestry. A particularly serious threat to these processes is posed by the movement of species, deliberately or

Answers and quick quizzes at **www.therevisionbutton.co.uk/myrevisionnotes**

accidentally, from one part of the world to another. **Exotic** or **alien species** can be introduced at any trophic level in the ecosystem. Often these introductions will prosper, but at the expense of native species. Their survival rates are enhanced by the fact that they lack native predators and are not susceptible to indigenous diseases. They are often more efficient competitors than native species. Examples of the deliberate introduction of exotic species that threaten biodiversity include the introduction of:

- game species for sporting purposes, e.g. pheasants, deer and rainbow trout
- plants such as rhododendron and Japanese knotweed

A similar situation occurs in the oceans with alien invasions by algae, crustaceans, insects and fish.

Now test yourself — Tested

10 What are the stores and pathways of an ecosystem? Include a sketch in your answer.

11 Why do exotic species often prosper?

Answers online

Impacts of economic development — Revised

When considering the impacts of economic development, it is important to distinguish between the destruction of a whole ecosystem or part of it and its degradation (decline in quality and biodiversity). Figure 3.3 shows the possible relationship between ecosystem state and economic development. In reality, the relationship is highly complicated. Much depends on the players and pressures (especially of population). The graph suggests that there might be some hope for threatened ecosystems if attempts are made to conserve them and move towards more sustainable use.

Typical mistake

Candidates often confuse the destruction of an ecosystem (e.g. by surface mining) with the more gradual degradation of an ecosystem (e.g. by over-exploitation or tourism).

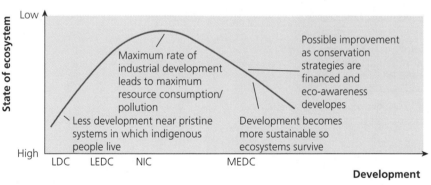

Figure 3.3 The possible relationship between ecosystem state and economic development

Now test yourself — Tested

12 What, if any, is the good news conveyed in Figure 3.3?

13 What is the difference between ecosystem destruction and degradation?

Answers online

Revision activity

List the different aspects of economic development that you think most threaten biodiversity.

Managing biodiversity

Sustainable yield

The concept of **sustainable yield** is a key one in relation to the sustainable management of ecosystems and biodiversity. Two levels of sustainable yield are recognised:

● Maximum sustainable yield (MSY) — the highest level of exploitation that can be sustained indefinitely and which will leave the ecosystem intact. Any 'harvesting' (exploitation) above this level is likely to threaten both species and their habitats. Strong commercial pressures often lead to this level of exploitation.

● Optimum sustainable yield (OSY) — a lower level of exploitation that does not spoil the aesthetic or recreational value of the ecosystem while at the same time allowing multi-use of the goods and services.

Another closely allied concept is that of **carrying capacity**. This is the maximum human population that can exist in equilibrium with the available resources of a given area. The problem with this is that carrying capacity varies seasonally and is expected to be reduced by climate change. Figure 3.4 shows the link between sustainable yield and carrying capacity. MSY is halfway between zero and carrying capacity.

> **Sustainable yield** is the level at which the goods and services of an ecosystem can be safely harvested without harming it.

> **Revision activity**
>
> Write brief notes about the concepts of sustainable yield and carrying capacity.

> **Now test yourself**
>
> 14 What is the link between sustainable yield and carrying capacity?
>
> Answer online
>
> Tested

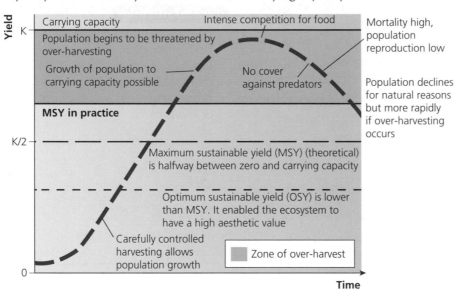

Figure 3.4 Sustainable yield

Key players

The key players that have some impact on whether and how biodiversity and ecosystems are managed are shown in Figure 3.5. It is clear that these players can be divided into two groups: those that have an impact at a global scale (e.g. TNCs, international NGOs and other organisations) and those that have an impact at a more local level (e.g. local communities, local government and individuals). The same players may also be divided into two groups on the basis of the nature of their impact on biodiversity management, i.e. whether it is negative (e.g. those concerned with exploitation) or whether it is positive (e.g. those pressing for conservation).

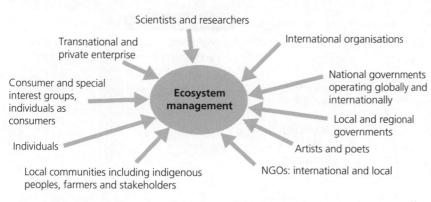

Figure 3.5 Players with an interest in ecosystem management

Now test yourself

15 Who are the key players with interests in the management of ecosystems and biodiversity?

Answer online

Tested

Revision activity

● List the key players in the field of managing ecosystems and biodiversity.
● Study Figure 3.5 and divide the players into two groups: those having negative impacts and those having positive impacts.

Strategies and policies

Revised

There is a range of possible conservation actions, from the total protection of areas and species to the **paper park** (a conservation area that exists solely on paper with no enforcement). The potential controversies surrounding the conservation of biodiversity and ecosystems centre around three specific issues:

● **What should be conserved?** As the funds available for conservation are limited, what projects should be given priority? A biodiversity hotspot strategy focuses on the most threatened of the high-quality areas, whereas an eco-region strategy conserves representative ecosystems. An iconic strategy prioritises particular high-profile species such as whales, tigers, penguins and condors, which is sometimes referred to as 'the cuddly-toy syndrome'. Keystone species deemed to have a particularly significant role in ecosystem health, such as bees, might be prioritised.

● **How should conservation take place?** There is a range of conservation actions along the spectrum, from total protection to total exploitation. Total protection strategies in the form of scientific reserves with no human access, created mainly in the 1960s, are subject to increasing criticism. In the twenty-first century, conservation seems to have moved on. Today, the fashion is to integrate conservation with economic development, but there are those who also criticise this approach because conserving biodiversity is often the second priority and economic development the first.

● **Which approach should be adopted?** There are tensions between top-down global strategies and local bottom-up initiatives. Indigenous people resent having schemes imposed on them from some distant authority. There is a need to integrate planning and actions at a variety of scales.

Revision activity

Note the three controversial issues that divide conservationists.

In an era of climate change, much attention is paid to the creation of large reserves (**biosphere reserves**) connected by open corridors running in a north–south direction. Such a layout facilitates the migration of species driven polewards by global warming. Two other points about biodiversity conservation need to be understood:

- *ex-situ* conservation has a role to play — for example, setting up seed and genetic banks in zoos and botanic gardens; captive breeding and release schemes
- conservation involves not only protection and management but also restoration of highly degraded ecosystems such as wetlands and forests

Now test yourself

Tested

16 What is the difference between the conservation of a biodiversity hotspot and the conservation of an eco-region?

17 What is the conservation spectrum?

Answers online

Uncertain futures

Revised

There are several factors that encourage uncertainty about future levels of biodiversity:

- the shortage of funding for protection and conservation, especially in developing countries
- the difficulty of properly policing protected areas — i.e. ensuring against the illegal exploitation of a particular species of plant or animal
- the rate at which biodiversity is being reduced outside protected areas
- the rate of future population growth and the likelihood of over-harvesting goods and services
- the degree of commitment to the cause of conservation — actions speak louder than words

Now test yourself

18 Identify some factors that give rise to uncertainty about future levels of biodiversity.

Answer online

Tested

Exam practice

Section A questions

1 The graph below shows biome loss between 1950 and 2050.

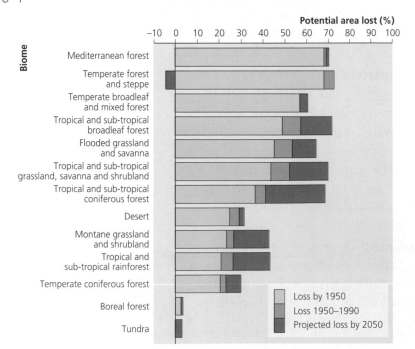

(a) Suggest reasons for the differences in biome losses between those up to 1990 and those projected to 2050. **[10]**

(b) Using examples, evaluate the global and local value of named ecosystems or biomes. **[15]**

2 The diagram below gives the IUCN Red List for 2008.

Holdridge's toad · Père David's deer · Little Earth hutia · Rameshwaram parachute spider · Iberian lynx · Cuban crocodile · Caspian seal · Fishing cat · Tasmanian devil

Becoming more endangered

Extinct or extinct in wild	Critically endangered, endangered and vulnerable	Near threatened	Of least concern

Becoming less endangered

Black-footed ferret · Wild horse · Walia ibex · Przewalski's gazelle · Arabian oryx · Indian rhinoceros · African elephant · Humpback whale

(a) Using the diagram and your own knowledge, explain how it is that some species on the Red List are becoming more endangered while others are now in less danger of extinction. **[10]**

(b) Evaluate the link between economic development and ecosystem destruction. **[15]**

Answers and quick quizzes online

Online

Examiner's summary

✔ Biodiversity is a resource in that it provides goods and services useful to humans. It has different components and varies considerably from place to place. In general, it declines with latitude.

✔ Biodiversity hotspots are recognised as areas that are very rich in species and are threatened by human activities. They occur both on land and in the sea. Together they account for a very small part of the globe's total area, but they contain significant percentages of the globe's floral and faunal species.

✔ The goods and services provided by ecosystems support different aspects of human wellbeing. The values of these goods and services vary from ecosystem to ecosystem and from user to user. Their use can often give rise to conflicts.

✔ A particular challenge for conservationists is to identify those areas where biodiversity is most threatened. At least four methods and measures have been devised. Between them they are capable of identifying two distinct types of area: threatened hotspots and areas containing threatened rare species.

✔ The threats to global biodiversity are both physical and human. Physical threats are mainly climate change and rising sea levels, whereas human threats are more diverse and include the impacts of different aspects of economic development and population growth.

✔ It is important to understand the processes of ecosystems, particularly energy flows and nutrient cycling. These are easily disrupted by a whole range of human activities from farming and urban growth to forestry and the introduction of exotic species. The impact of these and many other activities is either destruction or degradation.

✔ Sustainable yield and carrying capacity are important concepts that must be understood if we are to successfully manage and conserve ecosystems and biodiversity.

✔ The conservation of ecosystems and biodiversity is not helped by the fact that there are different and conflicting views on such basic issues as what and how to conserve, and which approach is better: top-down or bottom-up.

✔ Today sees the world's biodiversity and ecosystems under serious threat. Their future is made uncertain by a range of factors from the scale of future population growth to more practical matters such as the strength of the will to conserve, funding and the policing of protected areas.

4 Superpower geographies

So far as the geography of power is concerned, four points need to be understood:

- **power** is not evenly distributed. Some nations have a disproportionate influence over global and regional decision-making; others work within organisations such as the United Nations and economic blocs and, as a consequence, exercise little individual influence. They simply participate in power-sharing

- the present geography of power is the outcome of complex processes that are often deeply rooted in the past

- the distribution of power is constantly changing as some countries gain power and others lose it

- the nature of power can also change from direct control to a more subtle control and influence

A new generation of **superpowers** is emerging known as the BRICs (Brazil, Russia, India and China). They play an increasingly important role in the global economy. The prospect is one of increasing tensions between these newcomers and the present superpowers: the USA and the EU.

> **Power** is mostly of an economic, political and military nature. In some instances, power is also projected through culture.

> **Superpowers** are states or organisations with a dominant position in the international system. They have the ability to influence events in their own interests and project power on a worldwide scale to protect those interests. The term was first used during the Second World War to refer to the USA, the USSR and the British Empire.

Typical mistake
China and India are often thought of as similar, but they are not.

Examiner's tip
Learn some key facts about China and India, such as GDP per capita, literacy and poverty rates.

Revision activity
Create a two-column table. In column 1, list the key terms that occur in this section. In column 2, write a definition of each term. Add further key terms that occur throughout the topic.

Superpower geographies

The concept of a superpower

Three levels of global power are recognised (Figure 4.1):

1. **superpowers** — their power is primarily economic and military, e.g. the USA, the EU and, prior to its break-up in 1990, the Soviet Union

2. **emerging superpowers** — their power is often based on increasing economic importance and sometimes resources, e.g. Brazil, Russia, India, China and the oil-rich Gulf states

3. **regional powers** — their sphere of influence tends to be continental rather than global, e.g. Japan and South Africa

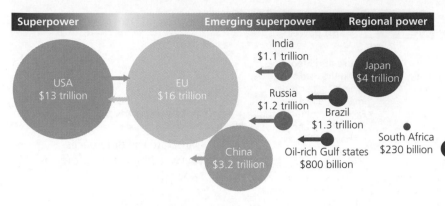

| Superpower | Emerging superpower | Regional power |

India $1.1 trillion

Japan $4 trillion

Russia $1.2 trillion

Brazil $1.3 trillion

South Africa $230 billion

USA $13 trillion

EU $16 trillion

China $3.2 trillion

Oil-rich Gulf states $800 billion

Figure 4.1 The global power spectrum and current trajectories, GDP data, 2008

Superpowers exercise various forms of power:

- **economic** — wealth and advanced development enable them to buy resources and influence trade patterns
- **military** — this is based on the possession of nuclear and other weapons, as well as monitoring the rest of the world by satellites and spy technology
- **cultural** — this influences the way people behave and involves the global promotion of a distinctive way of life and a particular set of values

Some superpowers also recognise what is called **geographical power**, but this is simply the sphere of influence of a superpower based on one or more of the above types of power.

Examiner's tip

Make sure you have learnt definitions of 'superpower' and 'emerging superpower' for the exam.

Typical mistake

Many candidates do not understand that the EU is a bloc whereas the USA is a nation state.

Revision activities

- Note the three different levels of global power and give an example of each.
- Develop your own 'index of power' using measures and/or data from the World Bank or UNDP.

Now test yourself

1 What are the main types of power exercised by a superpower?

Answer online

Tested

The geography of power and international influence

Revised

Superpowers maintain their influence in different ways, ranging from hard (overt) to soft (subtle) mechanisms (Figure 4.2):

- **Hard**: military means are the most threatening mechanisms. The USA has a military presence on all the continents except Antarctica. Its military power is strengthened by its membership of NATO (North Atlantic Treaty Organization), which provides it with allies in Europe.
- **Intermediate**: trade and aid figure here. Membership of trade blocs can do much to extend economic power with respect to resources, as well as both imports and exports. Aid is often given with 'strings attached' that favours the superpower donor.
- **Soft**: culture and ideology represent the soft end of the power spectrum. Here, the media play an important role in promoting images and messages. In many cases the promoted materials are little more than propaganda.

← Hard power   Soft power →

Military presence and force
- Large air, naval and land forces
- Nuclear weapons
- Military bases in foreign countries giving geographical reach
- Military alliances such as NATO
- Diplomatic threats to use force if negotiation fails, and the use of force

Aid and trade
- Favouring certain trade partners by reducing import tariffs
- Trade blocs and alliances
- Providing allies with economic and technical assistance
- Using aid to influence policy or keep allies happy
- Using economic sanctions against countries

Culture and ideology
- Using the media to promote a particular image and message
- Exporting culture in the form of film and TV, or globally recognised brands
- Gradually persuading doubters that a particular action or view is in their interests

Figure 4.2 The mechanisms of power

Now test yourself
2 Illustrate the differences between hard and soft forms of power.

Answer online

Tested

Changing patterns of power
Revised

History tells us that the geography or distribution of power has changed over time. Not only do old superpowers decline and new ones emerge, but the overall pattern can also change. Over the last 250 years, three different patterns or 'worlds' have occurred:

- a **unipolar pattern** with one dominant power, as was the case up to 1944 when the British Empire was the dominant global power
- a **bipolar pattern** in which two opposing superpowers exist, as was the case between 1945 and 1990 when the USA and the USSR challenged each other for global domination (the Cold War)
- a **multipolar pattern** of three or more superpowers, which seems to have been evolving since 2010. This involves the USA, the EU and China. Maybe the global power struggle between these countries will be joined by India and Russia

Examiner's tip
It is important to understand that there are different views about the present status of China. Some argue that it is already a superpower, while others see it as an emerging superpower along with the other BRICs.

Examiner's tip
You should learn a timeline of superpower change and be able to refer to the changing geography of power in terms of unipolar, bipolar and multipolar patterns.

Revision activities
- Draw a sketch to show the three different patterns of global power.
- Identify the powers involved in the change from a unipolar to a multipolar pattern during the twentieth century.

Now test yourself
3 Which sort of superpower pattern prevailed for much of the first half of the twentieth century?

Answer online

Tested

Theories
Revised

Several theories have been put forward to explain the existence of rich powerful countries and the poorer, weaker ones they dominate:

- **Modernisation theory** (W. W. Rostow) argues that the economies of developed countries move along a development pathway involving five stages. The British Empire was the first to experience the industrial revolution. This gave it an initial advantage over as yet unindustrialised countries and provided the basis for it becoming a superpower.
- **Dependency theory** (A. G. Frank) divides the world into an economically developed core and an underdeveloped periphery. The capitalist core (the superpowers) deliberately keeps the periphery in a state of underdevelopment. The core does this by exploiting the periphery's cheap resources and labour and by selling manufactured goods made in the core.

- **World-systems theory** (I. Wallerstein) recognises a three-tiered world: core, semi-periphery and periphery. It is a more dynamic model and contrasts with the distinctly static dependency model. It allows for countries to move up the tiers, i.e. from periphery to semi-periphery, from semi-periphery to core.

There are conflicting views about what is currently happening to the geography of global power. The controversy centres on the rise of China and India:

- World-systems theory argues that industrial capitalism (a superpower force) was born in Europe and that the rise of China and India simply represents another stage in the growth of the global economy. The theory also allows for superpowers to fall back, as with the break-up of the British Empire.

- Dependency theory views the rise of the two countries as simply a return to a much older world order when they were powerful economic forces. It therefore sees the UK and other European countries as the first NICs.

Neither theory explains why the global economic centre of gravity should shift, first from Asia to Europe and then back again.

Examiner's tip

Don't forget to refer to specific theories in the exam. Remember that these theories are also related to Topic 5, Bridging the development gap.

Now test yourself   Tested ☐

4   Summarise the main arguments in support of the three theories of modernisation, dependency and world-systems.

5   Which of the three theories do you favour most and why?

6   What are the two different views about the rise of China and India as global powers?

Answers online

Revision activity

Note the names of the three theories and write brief notes about the basic idea behind each of them.

The role of superpowers

Maintaining control ──────────────────────────── Revised ☐

The role of superpowers is essentially one of control in a way that promotes their best interests. Once gained, superpower status is maintained by the same power (economic, military, political or cultural) that promoted it. That power may be used to control territories, people, resources and markets.

Over the last 500 years or so, the world has witnessed two main types of control system. For much of that time, the system was **colonialism**, a direct form of control that involved:

- using, or threatening to use, military force
- imposing government systems run by administrators from the superpower
- imposing the laws, language and culture of the superpower
- creating a two-class society of the colonisers and the colonised

Colonialism is the acquisition, development and settlement of territory by another country.

This type of control was used to create and sustain the British Empire between the late sixteenth and the mid-twentieth centuries. At one time, the Empire extended over nearly a quarter of the world's land surface.

During the twentieth century, colonialism gave way to **neo-colonialism**. This system involves a form of indirect control by developed countries over developing countries. Control is less overtly military and cultural, but more economic. Control is exercised through:

- **aid**, which is most often given with 'strings attached', forcing recipient countries to use it in the way dictated by the donor countries
- **debt**, much of which is in the form of loans that have to be repaid with interest; default over repayments leads to increasing debt
- **TNCs**, which do much of the economic exploitation of resources, labour and markets by means of foreign direct investment
- **terms of trade**, which favour the superpower so that it enjoys cheap imports and high prices for its exports
- **strategic alliances**, which have a military basis in that superpowers offer 'protection' to their subservient developing countries

Perhaps the most blatant example of neo-colonialism today is China's move into Africa in search of resources (notably oil and copper) and markets for its manufactured goods.

> **Neo-colonialism** is the control of the economic and political systems of one country (usually a developing one) by a more powerful country (usually a developed one).

Examiner's tip

Be clear about the differences between colonialism and neo-colonialism. Colonialism involved direct control whereas neo-colonialism relies on indirect control.

Revision activities

- Compile a summary about the British Empire — its duration, its extent and its means of control.
- Make brief notes about the five ways in which neo-colonial power is implemented.
- List the costs and benefits of China's increasing investment in Africa from both China's and Africa's viewpoints.

Now test yourself

7 Summarise the differences between colonialism and neo-colonialism.

Answer online

Tested

International decision-making

Revised

Key decisions about the global economy, conflicts and environmental issues are made by the leaders of the superpowers and emerging superpowers through the medium of international organisations, especially intergovernmental organisations (IGOs). The main **players** are shown in Figure 4.3.

Examiner's tip

For the exam, you will need some examples of how these organisations influence what is going on in the world.

Figure 4.3 IGOs involved in global decision-making

Revision activity

List the names of international bodies through which the global powers exercise their control. Make notes about each body's sphere of influence.

Now test yourself

8 Name four IGOs through which global powers exercise control.

Answer online

Tested

Answers and quick quizzes at **www.therevisionbutton.co.uk/myrevisionnotes**

Trade

Trade is the buying, selling and exchange of goods and services. It is the generator of wealth; with wealth comes power. A large percentage of global trade is accounted for by the superpowers and emerging superpowers. They have significant advantages when it comes to world trade:

- they are the leading players in economic IGOs such as the powerful trade blocs of NAFTA, the EU and ASEAN
- many of the TNCs responsible for generating much world trade are located in those countries
- most major shipping lines and airlines are based in or operate out of those countries

The USA is at an advantage here in that the US dollar is the world's reserve currency. In short, trade plays an important part in creating and sustaining superpower status.

The **terms of trade** favour the strong. Many African countries are still trapped in a colonial-style trade pattern controlled by developed countries. They export low-value raw materials such as coffee, timber and copper. The prices of these and other commodities are set on global stock exchanges. As a result, they have no control over those prices. In return, they import costly manufactured goods.

> **Examiner's tip**
>
> IGOs are made up of sovereign states. They are established by treaty and, in most cases, represent powerful groupings of countries with common interests. The G8 and UN are two examples; so too are the trade blocs.

> **Typical mistake**
>
> Don't consider trade as only involving goods; services are also an important commodity.

> **Typical mistake**
>
> Many candidates believe that all TNCs are American. However, Shell (the Netherlands), AstraZeneca (the UK) and Toyota (Japan) are just three of the many exceptions to that mistaken generalisation.

> **Revision activity**
>
> Create a table to show which countries belong to NAFTA, the EU and ASEAN.

> **Now test yourself** Tested
>
> 9 In what ways do the terms of global trade favour developed countries?
>
> **Answer online**

Superpower culture

The dominance of the USA as a superpower, together with the power of the EU, has led to the identification of a **global culture** and the process of **cultural globalisation**. Among its distinguishing characteristics are a:

- culture of **consumerism**
- culture of **capitalism** and a belief in the importance of wealth
- belief in democracy and individualism
- belief that technology can solve most problems
- white Anglo-Saxon culture with English as the dominant language
- culture that 'cherry picks', adapts and absorbs selected parts of other cultures

Eight factors promoting cultural globalisation are shown in Figure 4.4.

> **Consumerism** is the belief that wealth and the ability to buy goods and services leads to happiness.
>
> **Capitalism** is the belief that production should be determined by private decisions rather than by state control.

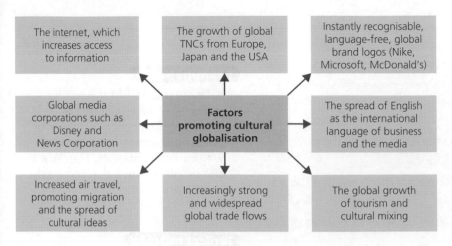

Figure 4.4 Factors promoting cultural globalisation

To many, global culture is more American than European, given the prominence of consumer icons such as Coca-Cola and McDonald's. Hollywood movies are also effective promoters of this Americanised global culture, as well as helping to sustain the USA's image as a superpower. However, not everyone is willing to accept the current form of global culture. There is a cultural backlash referred to as **anti-Americanism** — a reaction particularly to American values.

Now test yourself   Tested ☐

10 Explain the meaning of the terms 'consumerism', 'capitalism' and 'democracy'.

11 What is meant by the term 'cultural globalisation'?

12 What are the factors promoting cultural globalisation?

Answers online

Superpower futures

The rise of the BRICs ——————————————————————— Revised ☐

Brazil, Russia, India and China are all emerging superpowers and potential superpowers. Some argue that China is already one. The oil-rich states of the Middle East are also hoping to join the ranks. The economic growth being enjoyed by all these states is bringing a range of benefits:

● a reduction in the number of people living in poverty

● an increase in the size of the middle class

● better access to goods and improved services

However, within these apparently successful countries the benefits are not spread evenly across their territories. In China, there is a strong disparity between the prosperous, urban coastal zone and the poor rural interior. In India, the growing middle class is concentrated in cities and the southern states. The rise of the BRICs is also giving rise to further concerns:

● the accelerating demand for and consumption of energy and other resources

- the adverse impact on the environment — from global warming to localised pollution
- the uneven distribution of the benefits of economic growth — although the numbers in poverty may be declining, there is a widening gap between rich and poor

Revision activities

- Write brief notes about what underlies the growing influence of each of the emerging superpowers.
- Note the three concerns associated with the rise of the BRICs.
- Visit the Goldman Sachs website at www.goldmansachs/our-thinking/topics/brics/index.hmtl for more information on the BRICs.

Now test yourself Tested ☐

13 What are the benefits currently being enjoyed by the BRICs?

14 What benefits, if any, is the developing world gaining from the rise of the BRICs?

15 Why is it that the energy powers are growing stronger?

Answers online

Examiner's tip

It is important to recognise that the BRICs are four very different countries in terms of their resources, strengths and weaknesses. In the exam, you should show that you are aware of these differences. Resist the temptation to make general statements about the BRICs as a whole.

Examiner's tip

Today there are just over 800 vehicles per 1000 people in the USA. This compares with a figure of 80 per 1000 in China. Just think of the resources and environmental implications should China ever reach the US level.

Impacts on the old cores   Revised ☐

The rise of the emerging superpowers will have significant repercussions on the rest of the world. The shift in power is likely to be particularly uncomfortable for the EU, the USA and Japan. The global recession has already checked their economic growth. The emerging superpowers are also likely to add to their troubles and serious challenges lie ahead. These include:

- ensuring future supplies of energy and minerals
- creating a balanced economic base that does not rely too heavily on services
- maintaining the lead in space exploration
- curbing outsourcing, which ultimately erodes core jobs and prosperity
- rejuvenating ageing populations, i.e. ensuring an adequate supply of labour and innovation
- preventing the spread and deployment of nuclear weapons

Now test yourself Tested ☐

16 In what ways do the emerging superpowers threaten the old core countries?

Answer online

Examiner's tip

Don't forget the demographic situation in the old and emerging superpowers. Ageing populations are an issue in the EU, Japan, Russia and China. In contrast, the USA, Brazil and India have much more youthful and expanding populations.

Typical mistake

It is incorrect to say that the USA is on the way out as a superpower — it is still the world's leading economy and commands great military strength and political power.

Revision activity

List the six challenges facing the EU, the USA and Japan.

Impacts elsewhere

Despite the rise of the BRICs, most of the world still belongs to the developing South. Some hope that their rise will create new opportunities for the developing world. The reality is that the developing world continues to be the victim of **neo-colonialism**. Its resources are exploited at an ever-increasing rate to meet the development demands of the BRICs. The developing world is reaping few benefits because the capital it receives from the export of resources hardly pays for imports of manufactured goods and services.

Rising tensions

A new world order seems to be emerging and most likely it will be a multipolar one. It is likely to comprise:

- the **present superpowers**, i.e. the EU and the USA
- the **emerging superpowers**, i.e. Brazil, China and India
- the **energy powers** — those countries that have large reserves of oil and gas such as Russia and the Middle Eastern states

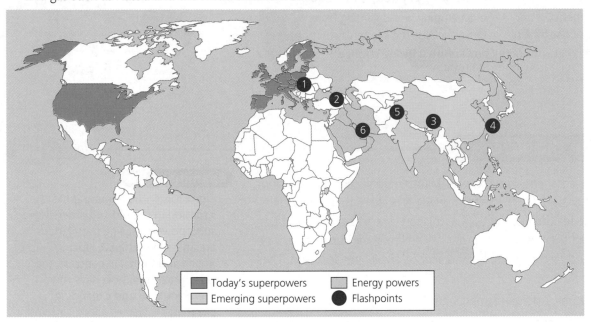

| Today's superpowers | Energy powers |
| Emerging superpowers | ● Flashpoints |

1 Ukrainian moves to join the EU or NATO may prompt Russia to disrupt gas flows to Europe
2 Georgia may press for NATO membership, increasing tensions in the Caucasus
3 China and India have an unresolved border dispute in South Tibet
4 The future of Taiwan, North Korea's nuclear weapons and the dispute over the Kuril Islands between Japan and Russia are all potential conflict sources
5 The unresolved Kashmir dispute could lead to conflict between India and Pakistan
6 Iraq, a nuclear-armed Iran and terrorism could all ignite tensions in the Persian Gulf

Figure 4.5 A multipolar world?

Increased tensions are likely because:

- there will be no dominant superpower and all powers will strive to prove their superiority, perhaps through their military might
- Brazil and the energy powers possess vital resources that other powers will want

> **Examiner's tip**
>
> Make sure you are able to recall the detail of at least three of these flashpoints.

Answers and quick quizzes at **www.therevisionbutton.co.uk/myrevisionnotes**

- any bilateral agreements between two powers are likely to provoke strong reactions
- the emerging superpowers are likely to encroach on the traditional spheres of influence of existing superpowers

Figure 4.5 shows six **flashpoints** or locations of particularly high tension. To that list one should add the cultural tensions between four different worlds (US corporate capitalism, European liberalism, the Islamic world and Chinese Confucianism). For example, there is the tension between the West and Islamic fundamentalism and the tensions in China as more and more of the population demand European-style freedoms.

Examiner's tip

Remember that the futures of all superpowers are uncertain. There is scope for you to advance your own views on those futures, provided you justify your views.

Now test yourself   Tested

17 Why is it expected that the emerging multipolar world could lead to a future of increasing tensions?

18 What underlies the tension between the West and the Islamic world?

Answers online

Revision activity

Make notes on three of the flashpoints shown in Figure 4.5.

Exam practice

Section A questions

1 Maps **A** and **B** below show contrasting models of wealth and power.

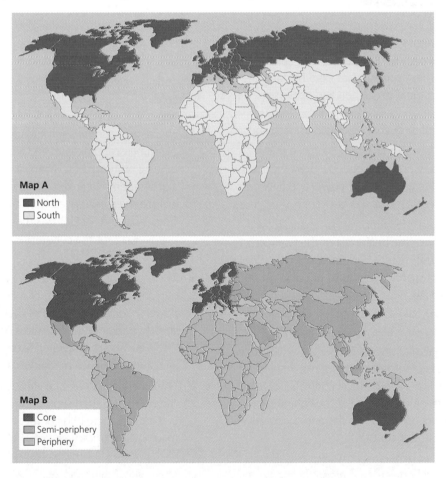

Map A
- North
- South

Map B
- Core
- Semi-periphery
- Periphery

(a) Explain how the two models reflect changing views of superpower status.   [10]

(b) Assess the roles of trade and international organisations in maintaining superpower status.   [15]

2 The table below compares China and the USA (data from 2009/10).

	China	Feature	USA	
★ ★ ★	1330 million	**Population**	310 million	★
★ ★ ★	7.7 billion tonnes	**CO_2 emissions**	5.4 billion tonnes	★ ★
★ ★ ★	2.2 million	**Active military personnel**	1.6 million	★ ★
★ ★ ★	$1500 billion	**Exports**	$1270 billion	★ ★
★ ★	251	**Embassies abroad**	289	★ ★ ★
★	$3700	**GDP per capita**	$45000	★ ★ ★
★ ★ ★	9.6%	**GDP growth**	2.6%	★
★	200 million Qzone	**Social media worldwide**	500 million Facebook	★ ★ ★
★	$0.7 billion	**Film industry**	$10.9 billion	★ ★ ★
★	Sinopec $187 billion	**Top brand and revenue**	Walmart $408 billion	★ ★ ★

(a) Using the figures and your own knowledge, explain why some people consider that the world is once again bipolar in terms of superpower geography. [10]

(b) Evaluate the likely impact of a multipolar superpower world on people and the planet. [15]

Answers and quick quizzes online

Online

Examiner's summary

✔ Three levels of global power are recognised: superpower, emerging superpower and regional power. Superpowers exert their influence in a variety of different ways. The spectrum runs from hard military control to soft cultural persuasion and conversion. In between, there are various forms of moderate economic control through media such as trade and aid.

✔ Theories have been put forward to explain the emergence of very powerful nations. How is it that they gain the different forms of power and how do they use it to dominate weaker countries?

✔ The distribution of global power has changed over the centuries. Since the beginning of the twentieth century, the global pattern has changed from unipolar to multipolar through a transitional phase when the pattern was bipolar.

✔ Over the last 500 years, the world has witnessed two slightly different control systems: colonialism and neo-colonialism. Both are inherently exploitative. Colonialism, as exemplified by the British Empire, involved the military and political control of large areas and imposing the culture of the colonial power. Neo-colonialism prevails to this day and it involves a more indirect form of control.

✔ Trade is not only a generator of wealth; it is also used by the global powers to exercise their influence and control. They are able to manipulate the terms of trade in their favour and in such a way that the weaker countries remain exploited and weak. The

global powers also exercise control through their leadership of international organisations such as the UN, the WTO, the World Bank and the IMF.

✔ Today's world is increasingly experiencing a global culture. This global culture is a fusion of Western values and aspects of the American way of life. With English as its dominant language, it is characterised by consumerism, capitalism and a belief in democracy. It is being promoted by what is referred to as cultural globalisation. Material symbols of this globalisation include the spread of commercial brands such as Coca-Cola and McDonald's, but not all the world is happy to adopt the culture. Resistance is strong in the Islamic world.

✔ The most notable event today in the changing pattern of global power is the rise of the BRICs (the emerging powers). Some regard one of them, China, as having already graduated to the status of a superpower. There are also the energy powers, which command increasing influence as reserves of oil and gas dwindle.

✔ The emerging powers are already having an impact on the two established superpowers (the USA and the EU), such as increased competition for resources and a matching of military power. The less-developed parts of the world continue to be exploited.

✔ The gradual shift in global power to a multipolar pattern is leading to an era of increasing tensions. Those tensions heighten the importance of military power.

5 Bridging the development gap

The **development gap** is the widening income and quality of life gap between the global 'haves' (the traditional and rising superpowers) of the developed world and the 'have-nots' (the poorest, least-developed countries) of the developing world. Three further points should be borne in mind:

- Development is seen as having two faces: economic development (a growth in wealth) and human development (an improvement in the quality of life, standard of living etc.).
- The majority view is that the global development gap is currently widening.
- Development gaps also exist within individual countries, for example between rural and urban areas, between regions or on the basis of gender or ethnicity.

To date, closing or bridging the development gap has proved a bridge too far. Clearly, the challenge facing global society is to find effective ways of elevating countries and peoples out of poverty.

> The **development gap** is the disparity in income and quality of life between the rich (more economically developed) and poor (less economically developed) countries.

> **Revision activity**
>
> Create a two-column table. In column 1, list the key terms that occur in this section. In column 2, write a definition of each term. Add further key terms that occur throughout the topic.

The causes of the development gap

Measuring the development gap — Revised

Economic development is measured by either gross domestic product (**GDP**) per capita or gross national income (**GNI**) per capita. Neither provides a perfect measure, so international comparisons based on them have to be used with caution.

A global map based on GDP per capita in 1981 suggested that there were two distinct 'worlds': the wealthy 'North' (mainly in the Northern Hemisphere) and the poorer 'South' (mainly in the Southern Hemisphere). The boundary separating them was known as the North–South (Brandt) line. Later, this twofold classification was refined by the World Bank. Figure 5.1 shows the global situation in the early part of this millennium.

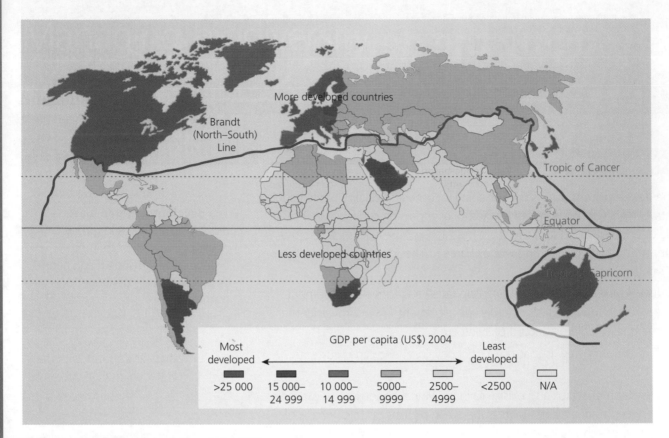

More developed countries

Brandt
(North–South)
Line

Tropic of Cancer

Equator

Less developed countries

Tropic of Capricorn

	GDP per capita (US$) 2004		
Most developed ←		→ Least developed
>25 000	15 000–24 999	10 000–14 999	5000–9999	2500–4999	<2500	N/A

Figure 5.1 Global distribution of per capita GDP

Typical mistake

The two measures — GDP and GNI — are not the same. GDP refers to the value of all goods and services produced by a country's economy during 1 year. GNI is GDP *plus* all the income that a country also earns during the same year from investments abroad. When both measures are expressed in per capita terms (i.e. divided by the number of people in a country's population), they provide two different measures of economic productivity and a sound basis for comparing countries.

Typical mistake

Many candidates think that the North–South line today is exactly the same as it was in the 1980s. Its precise course has changed and, because of the emergent economies, it is less stark as a boundary.

Human development is measured by the Human Development Index (**HDI**), which takes into account three critical aspects of wellbeing:

- life expectancy
- literacy
- GDP per capita

Examiner's tip

Remember that Millennium Development Goals have been set only for developing countries.

Other possible measures of development include the **Physical Quality of Life Index** (**PQLI**), the **Gender-related Development Index** (**GDI**) and the **Technology Achievement Index** (**TAI**). The **Millennium Development Goals** (**MDGs**) are useful in terms of measuring what is happening to the development gap — whether it is widening or reducing. There are eight goals and the aim is to achieve them by 2015. Specific MDG targets include eradicating extreme poverty, promoting gender equality, improving health and combating contagious diseases, as well as ensuring environmental sustainability.

Revision activity

Redraw the North–South line in Figure 5.1 to show where you think the boundary between North and South runs today.

Answers and quick quizzes at **www.therevisionbutton.co.uk/myrevisionnotes**

Now test yourself

Tested

1 What is the difference between economic development and human development?
2 What measures are used to assess the state of human development?

Answers online

Theoretical explanations

Revised

Several theories have been put forward to explain the existence of rich powerful countries and the poorer, weaker ones that they dominate:

- **Modernisation theory** (W. W. Rostow) argues that the economies of developed countries move along a development pathway involving five stages. The British Empire was the first to experience the industrial revolution. This gave it an initial advantage over as yet unindustrialised countries.
- **Core-periphery theory** (J. Friedmann) divides the world into developed core regions and less developed peripheral regions. The development process favours the core regions at the expense of the periphery, thus widening the development gap.
- **Dependency theory** (A. G. Frank) is somewhat similar to the core-periphery theory and divides the world into an economically developed core and an underdeveloped periphery. The capitalist core deliberately keeps the periphery in a state of underdevelopment. The core does this by exploiting the periphery's cheap resources and labour and by selling manufactured goods made in the core.
- **Poverty theory** focuses on underdevelopment and explains it in terms of poverty and deprivation. Less developed countries are trapped in a vicious circle of poverty by a lack of capital and low incomes. However, this theory cannot account for the sudden appearance of the emergent economies — countries that have managed somehow to break out of the circle.
- **Debt theory** is similar to poverty theory, but it considers underdeveloped countries as trapped in a cycle of debt. In the past, many poor countries have accepted loans from rich countries. These have to be repaid, together with interest. Subsequent default on repayment has led to increasing debt.

Examiner's tip

You should be able to refer to specific theories in your exam answers.

Revision activity

Note the differences between core-periphery theory and dependency theory.

Now test yourself

Tested

3 Which of the five theories do you think best explains the existence of the development gap?

Answer online

Global players

Revised

The major players in global development are shown in Figure 5.2.

Figure 5.2 Major players in global development

These major players divide roughly into two camps:

- those that aim to reduce the development gap — the UN, WTO and BINGOs
- those that aim to maintain the development gap — the TNCs and superpowers

Examiner's tip

Check that you understand the particular roles played by each organisation.

Now test yourself

Tested

4 Which specific organisations do you think aim to reduce the development gap?

Answer online

Trade and investment

Revised

Trade and investment play a key role in the workings of the global economy. For this reason, they impact on the development gap.

Broadly speaking, the world prices for primary products have fallen over recent years in relation to the price of manufactured goods. Therefore, countries that export such products and import manufactured goods are suffering from declining **terms of trade**. This is often the situation with the poorest countries. It leads to a decline in living standards and an increase in poverty. The impact is likely to widen the development gap. It certainly helps to sustain the superior wealth of developed countries.

Terms of trade is the ratio between the income earned by a country's exports and the prices of its imports.

Here are two examples of global trade patterns of primary products:

- Coffee is grown mainly in tropical and subtropical areas of Latin America, Asia and Africa. Its main markets are in the high-income countries of Europe, North America, Australia and Japan. The coffee industry's supply chain involves growers, middlemen, exporters, importers, roasters and retailers before the product reaches the consumer.

- Bananas are also grown in tropical and subtropical areas, but mainly in Latin America and the Caribbean. Only 15% of the global banana crop is exported, largely to high-income countries. Most of the global banana trade is in the hands of five TNCs: Chiquita, Dole, Del Monte, Noboa and Fyffes.

Traditionally, global **trade flows** have been between the North and the South. The developing countries of the South have exported primary products such as agricultural products and minerals to the North. More recently, however, developing countries (especially NICs) have capitalised on their cheap labour and moved into manufacturing. Manufactured goods are now prominent in their exports.

The crucial aspect of trade is the **balance of trade**. Countries have either **trade surpluses** (when exports exceed imports) or **trade deficits** (when imports exceed exports). Trade deficits are bad news, particularly for developing countries, because they can so easily lead to a **debt trap** that stifles investment and economic growth.

The **balance of trade** is the difference between a country's exports and imports in terms of value or volume.

The **debt trap** is an arrangement whereby a developing country accepts a long-term loan as aid, but under terms that favour the lender country. Default on repayment or payment of interest can lead easily into a vicious circle of increasing debt.

Now test yourself

Tested

5 Why is trade important in the workings of the global economy?
6 What is the significance of the following?
   (a) terms of trade
   (b) balance of trade

Answers online

Revision activities

- Research the distribution of global trade at a regional level by value of exports.
- Draw an annotated diagram showing the supply chain of either coffee or bananas.

The consequences of the development gap

Impact on people in disadvantaged countries

Revised

The existence of the development gap has a range of consequences — social, economic, political and environmental — not just for whole countries but within them for regions and groups of people.

As with countries, the development gap means that there are both 'winners' and 'losers'. The argument is that the 'losers' in poor countries fare far worse than those in rich countries. There are three particularly disadvantaged groups of people:

- People living in remote rural areas are trapped in the cycle of poverty, which is rooted in the inability to produce enough food and find other resources like fuel and water.

- Members of low castes are also trapped in a social system that denies them any hope of social upward mobility. They also find it difficult to access public facilities and services, such as schools and healthcare. The caste system in India designates that all people belonging to a particular caste follow the same trade. A person remains a member of the caste into which they are born and is usually debarred from social contact with people from other castes. The caste system has begun to weaken in the growing urban areas of India. Ethnic or religious minority groups often experience a similar situation.

● Women in developing countries are more likely than men to be unpaid family workers or have low-status jobs with lower wages. They are often trapped in the home and debarred from participation in politics and government. This, in turn, means that they are able to do little in terms of pressing for gender equality.

In short, within the populations of every country there are disadvantaged groups. Even in developed countries there are groups such as people with a disability and those belonging to ethnic and religious minorities. All are bypassed by the positive impacts of development.

Revision activity

Explain the reasons why remote rural areas lag behind in terms of development.

Now test yourself   Tested ☐

7 How does the caste system prevent social mobility?
8 Why is it that in many developing countries women are, in effect, second-class citizens?

Answers online

The poor in megacities   Revised ☐

As development begins to take off in poorer countries, there is rapid urbanisation largely fuelled by huge volumes of rural-to-urban migration. This leads to the growth of **megacities** such as Cairo (Egypt), Nairobi (Kenya), Dhaka (Bangladesh) and Bangkok (Thailand). The widespread perception is that the key to a better future can be found in huge cities such as these.

Unfortunately, in the early stages of their growth the traditional poverty of rural areas is simply transferred to urban **slums**, usually referred to as **shanty towns**. These tracts of substandard housing are a reminder of high levels of inequality between poor and rich. They are testimony to the fact that the demand for housing outstrips supply. This, in turn, causes the costs of housing to rise far above the earning power of most newly arrived workers. The slums become home to great poverty and deprivation, from which there is little escape.

Considerable **environmental costs** are a major downside to the emergence of megacities. The effects are often so bad and widespread that they impact even on the rich. The costs include air and water pollution, deficient water supplies and inadequate waste disposal.

It is possible to classify the megacities of the developing world according to their general state of development:

● **immature** (Kabul, Lagos) — much informal trading; high incidence of poverty; much environmental pollution; difficult to govern
● **consolidating** (Dhaka, Nairobi) — growing employment in manufacturing and services; some upgrading of slums; still high levels of environmental damage; some semblance of city government

Megacities are cities with a population of over 10 million. There are 27 megacities worldwide, with 15 of these in Asia.

Examiner's tip

You need to know some examples of poor rural areas that are being drained of people by rural-to-urban migration.

Shanty towns are makeshift dwellings built of scrap materials on tracts of waste or unused land and usually lacking basic services such as water, sanitation and lighting.

Examiner's tip

Although there is much poverty in the least developed countries, not everyone is poor. In all of these countries there is a wealthy elite, although admittedly a small one.

- **maturing** (Mexico City, Mumbai) — upgrading of services; population growth rate slows; environmental problems being tackled; growing political tensions between rich and poor

Examiner's tip

In your answers, refer to specific megacities and go easy on broad generalisations about all megacities.

Revision activity

Make notes about one exemplar megacity for each of the three types.

Now test yourself   Tested ☐

9 Why are megacities in the developing world growing so quickly?

10 Why do these megacities contain so much poverty?

Answers online

Typical mistake

Too many candidates refer to Africa as a country, but it is a continent occupied by a number of countries.

Ethnic and religious dimensions   Revised ☐

Figure 5.3 gives some examples of disadvantaged groups for whom the development gap has had some negative consequences. All but one of them (disabled/old people) has an ethnic or religious dimension, even the contract migrant workers.

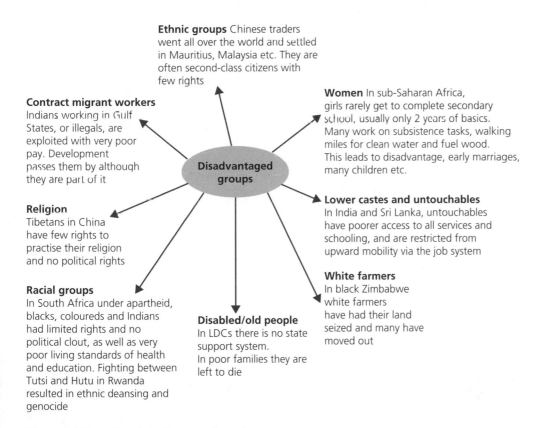

Figure 5.3 Examples of disadvantaged groups

It is easy to understand how disparities in wealth can generate discrimination and unrest between the 'haves' and the 'have-nots', especially when they align with differences in ethnicity, religion, class or political allegiance. This is well illustrated by the experiences of apartheid in South Africa and the Indonesian occupation of East Timor. The Arab Spring in North Africa and the Middle East during 2011 is an example of people (young men and women, members of minority tribes) rising up against discrimination and a wealthy political elite.

Revision activity

Make notes about the tribal differences within one of the countries involved in the Arab Spring.

Positive and negative consequences of development

Revised

Table 5.1 shows the positive and negative impacts of development as countries such as the BRICs make their way across the global development gap and out of poverty.

Table 5.1 Consequences for countries crossing the development gap

Positive impacts	Negative impacts
• Increased investment from foreign direct investment (FDI) and internally • Rising personal incomes from an improved range of employment • Improved education and a more skilled population • New projects to extend infrastructure — some high profile schemes extend the influence of the country • Improved international status, membership of WTO etc. • Expansion in core cities should trickle down to the periphery and the poor • Increasingly 'switched on' by the technology of mobile phones/the internet	• Over-reliance on export-led growth • Increasing indebtness to international banks for loans • Increasing reliance on TNCs, which can dominate decision-making • Increasing pressure on services such as waste, health and education • Increasing pressure on land and ecosystems because of expanding development • Increasing pressure on resources for energy • Increasing levels of air and water pollution from industrialisation • Increasing congestion from traffic • Attraction of migrant workers compounds these environmental pressures • Pressure on cultural traditions and values

In general, we might conclude from Table 5.1 that the positives are largely economic and to a lesser extent social. In contrast, the negatives are environmental and, perhaps surprisingly, also economic.

Revision activities

- Compare the development pathways of China and India.
- Group the positives and negatives in Table 5.1 under the headings economic, social and environmental.

Now test yourself

Tested

11 Why are the positive impacts of development not shared by all?

12 What are the negative environmental impacts experienced by the emergent economies?

Answers online

Reducing the development gap

Theories and approaches

Revised

Some of the theories put forward to explain the origins of the development gap may also be applied to the task of finding ways of reducing it:

- **Modernisation** suggests that, given time, all developing countries can follow the path of industrialised ones. In short, there will come a time when the gap disappears, but perhaps this is rather naive and optimistic.
- **Neo-liberalism** focuses on globalisation and the growth of the global economy. It argues that this approach offers opportunities for all. It is quick to point out that the development gap has already been crossed by the first NICs (Singapore, South Korean, Taiwan and Hong Kong)

and that it is currently being bridged by the BRICs (Brazil, Russia, India and China).

- **Marxism** argues it is only government action that can narrow the gap, which requires a top-down approach by highly centralised, communist governments. This was the approach taken in Cuba.
- **Populism** suggests the very opposite, i.e. a left-wing, grass-roots, bottom-up approach to development.
- **Post-development theory** looks to NGOs and a pragmatic approach. This puts the emphasis on sustainable development and small-scale, local projects using intermediate technology.

Figure 5.4 takes a more practical view and suggests that there are two sets of actions or approaches for closing the gap. It is these that need to be combined into coherent strategies.

Examiner's tip

Remember the five stages of Rostow's modernisation theory, which provide a useful framework for looking at the economic development of countries.

Revision activity

Familiarise yourself with the thinking behind populism and post-development theory.

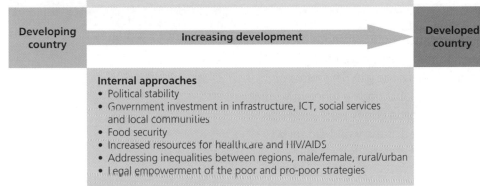

Figure 5.4 Routes to closing the development gap

Now test yourself   Tested ☐

13 What are the limitations of modernisation and neo-liberalism in terms of closing the development gap?

14 What is the difference between a Marxist and a populist approach to development?

Answers online

Aid strategies   Revised ☐

It is widely agreed that closing the development gap will require developed countries reaching across it and extending aid in various forms. All aid falls into one of two types: top-down or bottom-up:

- **Top-down aid** — the donor country transfers resources either to a multilateral aid organisation such as the UN or directly to the government of a receiving country that takes responsibility for allocating and distributing those resources. Aid can take various forms such as grants, loans, machinery, weapons, technology and technicians. There are risks associated with this type of aid: it is often tied, i.e. it comes with 'strings attached' that are to the advantage of the donor country; because of corruption, the aid sometimes does not reach the most deserving areas and the poorest people. Also open to criticism are other forms of top-down aid: the capital-intensive, megaprojects of the World Bank, along with IMF loans, can actually impede development.

- **Bottom-up aid** — this is the route favoured by many NGOs. It is targeted at the most needy and usually takes the form of local projects. Such projects are typically small scale, slow to reach many people and financially vulnerable.

A criticism of both forms of aid is that they are aimed at the symptoms of poverty not its causes. Does aid really help a country to stand on its own two feet?

Now test yourself   Tested ☐

15 How is it that aid impedes development?

Answer online

Trade and investment ————————————————— Revised ☐

As a means of reducing the development gap, trade is perhaps even more controversial. Neo-liberalism argues that trade helps poor countries develop. An opposite view is that trade widens the gap. The terms of trade favour more developed countries, so global trade is inherently unfair. Trade blocs, protectionist policies and controlled commodity prices are among the obstacles that need to be removed. If the world did move towards a fairer and freer trade, there might be grounds for a mild optimism about the prospects for poorer countries. The **fair trade** movement started in the 1960s continues to stand as an example of the way global trade should be conducted.

Unlike aid, investment is undertaken with the expectation of financial return. TNCs are the main sources of FDI and they invest for profit. The countries in which they invest benefit in some small ways (such as jobs and exports), but the benefits are nowhere near the scale of those reaped by the investor. In general, investment is not contributing much to narrowing the development gap.

Now test yourself   Tested ☐

16 What is the difference between trade and FDI?
17 Why are trade and FDI doing so little to close the development gap?

Answers online

Future actions ————————————————————— Revised ☐

Although there are indicators (e.g. the MDGs) that some advances have been made in the global battle against poverty, there is little to indicate any closing of the development gap. It is true that some countries have crossed it, while others are in the process of doing so. The sobering fact is that although poorer countries might take tentative steps along the development pathway, wealthy countries are striding away and ahead along the same pathway. The chances of any catch-up are fairly remote. Given the conclusion that aid, trade and investment are doing little at present to close the gap, should the following possible actions be considered?

● **debt cancellation** — many poor countries are overburdened by debts accumulated as a result of aid loans. Wiping the slate clean would certainly increase their chances

● **tourism** — many countries have the resources (scenery, biodiversity, recreational opportunities) to attract tourists from developed countries. Tourism can generate a beneficial multiplier effect

● **technology** — the spread of ICT, especially mobile phones and the internet, could play a significant part in promoting bottom-up developments

● **legal rights** — insuring such things as property and labour rights, as well as access to justice, would do much to empower the poor to improve their lot

● **cooperation in the South** — this is based on the idea that poor nations might find appropriate low-cost and sustainable solutions to their problems in other developing countries rather than in the rich North

None of these on its own provides a 'silver bullet' solution, but together they might bring about some closure of the development gap.

Examiner's tip

You need to learn specific located examples of the five possible future actions.

Revision activities

● Get up-to-date information about progress towards the MDGs by visiting www.un.org/millenniumgoals/pdf/.

● Investigate the two sides of the argument about debt cancellation.

Now test yourself

18 Which of the five possible catch-up actions do you think is likely to work best? Give your reasons.

Answer online

Tested ☐

Exam practice

Section A questions

1 The diagram below shows development differences in Pakistan and Guatemala.

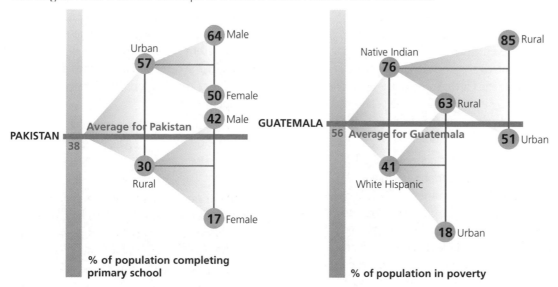

(a) Explain why some groups of people within countries have different levels of development. [10]

(b) Using examples, evaluate the usefulness of different ways of measuring development. [15]

2 The graph below shows how the income groups of various countries have changed since 1820.

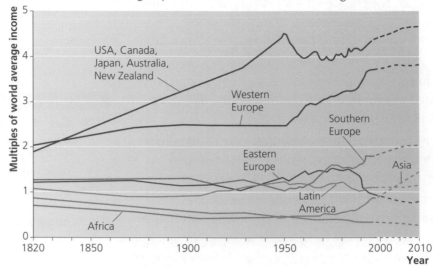

(a) Explain how it is that the graph shows conflicting evidence of what has happened to the development gap since 1950. [10]

(b) Evaluate the role of aid in bridging the development gap. [15]

Answers and quick quizzes online

Online

Examiner's summary

✔ The countries of today's world largely fall into two categories: the wealthy (the 'haves') and the poor (the 'have-nots'). They are separated by the development gap. The existence of this gap is revealed by economic (GDP per capita) and quality of life indicators (literacy rates).

✔ A number of theories have been put forward to explain the origins and persistence of the development gap. The broad argument is that the gap arises from different social, economic and political systems that prevent wealth and advantage being evenly spread across the Earth. Some of these theories are also challenged by the fact that some countries have managed to cross the gap (the first NICs) and others (the BRICs) are currently doing so.

✔ There are a number of different players involved in the growth of the global economy, including the World Bank, the IMF, governments, TNCs and NGOs. Although all claim to be committed to the closure of the development gap, their actions do not always achieve this. For example, it is claimed that involvement in global trade gives poorer countries a chance to develop, but the terms of trade are such that they favour developed rather than developing countries.

✔ Development gaps also exist within countries (between core and peripheral regions, between urban and rural areas) and between groups of people (rich and poor, gender, ethnic and religious minorities). The discrimination involved here causes tensions that can lead to unrest and uprisings. This discrimination seems to be most marked in poorer countries.

✔ A paradox is to be found in the emerging megacities of developing countries. They are to be seen as spearheading a country's development and yet they contain huge pockets of poverty. These pockets simply represent the concentrations of the rural poor attracted by the perceived attractions of urban life. What most of them do not find is decent housing and properly paid work.

✔ For those countries that have made or are making it across the development gap, progress is not all positive. There are some clear negatives, both environmental and economic.

✔ Just as there are theories to explain the development gap, so too there are theories as to how best to close the gap. Of these, the populist and post-development approaches would seem to have most to offer.

✔ Most see the narrowing of the development gap as being brought about by aid, trade and investment, but it is clear that they do not always work in the desired way. It is vital that we look to other possible actions, such as debt cancellation, tourism, technology and more cooperation in the South.

6 The technological fix?

Key concepts   Revised

Access to **technology** is an integral part of development. It allows people to control their environment and improve their quality of life. Use of technology brings benefits that are mainly economic and to a lesser degree social. However, it also brings costs that are largely social and environmental.

Many people believe there is a technological fix for every problem and that it is only a matter of time before a solution is found. However, problems can also be solved by changes in human attitudes and behaviour. Access to technology varies from place to place and there are deep-seated disparities.

> **Technology** is the invention and use of tools, machines, systems and procedures in order to perform a particular function, solve a problem or improve a pre-existing solution to a problem.

Examiner's tip

Make sure you learn the definition of technology for the exam.

Revision activity

Create a two-column table. In column 1, list the key terms that occur in this section. In column 2, write a definition of each term. Add further key terms that occur throughout the topic.

The geography of technology

Defining technology   Revised

Invention, innovation and the control of nature lie at the heart of technology. It increases the ability of people to satisfy their needs, for example by:

- controlling the environment, e.g. crop irrigation and flood protection schemes
- increasing food production by crop and livestock breeding, mechanisation and the design and application of fertilisers and pesticides
- raising manufacturing output by new machines, automation and more efficient production systems
- inventing new and faster ways of moving people and commodities (by transport) and communicating (by information technology)
- extending life expectancy with new medicines and treatments
- raising the ability to attack and defend territory and people by military weaponry

Examiner's tip

Don't write vaguely about cars and computers as examples of modern technology — try to be specific.

Revision activity

Find specific examples of each of the six ways technology is helping to meet human needs.

Now test yourself   Tested

1   Give six ways in which technology can satisfy human needs.

Answer online

Geographical distribution

The global distributions of technology and the pattern of dependence on it are not even. This disparity occurs because of the close links between economic development and technology. Developed countries:

● make most use of technology

● depend most on technology

● are the sources of many of the advances in technology

● are the first to benefit from it

For example, developed countries were the first to benefit from the huge leaps forward in communications technology. The traditional North–South divide in development is well reflected in the distribution of internet users (Figure 6.1). Over much of Africa and Asia, less than 20% of the population are internet users. In North America, Western Europe and Australia, the figure is over 60%. Electricity is needed for running many forms of modern technology and yet there are still large areas of the developing world without it.

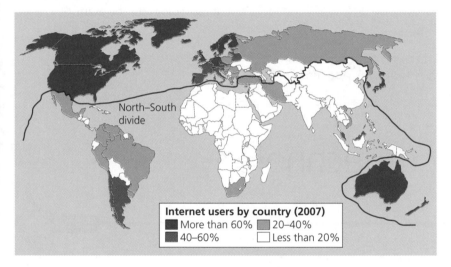

North–South divide

Internet users by country (2007)
More than 60%   20–40%
40–60%   Less than 20%

Figure 6.1 Global distribution of internet access, 2007

It would be wrong, however, to think that developing countries do not benefit from technology. There is a trickling down of new technology from developed countries. For example, developing countries are benefiting from some of the advances listed in Topic 5: from some aspects of environmental control to new ways of raising food production. Improvements in transport are now connecting even the most remote countries to the global economy.

Revision activity

Research and update Figure 6.1. You might also check out global access to electricity.

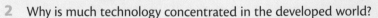

Now test yourself

Tested

2 Why is much technology concentrated in the developed world?

3 Why is electricity a factor affecting access to technology?

4 Give some examples where the incidence of internet users does not coincide with the North–South divide.

Answers online

Access to technology

Wealth and level of development explain why some parts of the world are at the cutting edge of new technologies, whereas others lack even the most basic access to technology. Money is undoubtedly a key requirement, but access to technology also requires:

● establishing the level of need and the potential benefits to be gained

● understanding how to make best use of it

● being able to maintain it properly

All three points perhaps emphasise the importance of education and skills as a prerequisite to the adoption of many forms of new technology.

Those countries with virtually no access to technology suffer from what is known as **environmental determinism**. This means that they are vulnerable to any challenge that the environment might present such as floods, drought, earthquakes or volcanic eruptions. Although technology cannot provide complete protection from such natural hazards, it can help in various ways to reduce the impact, from prediction to **adjustment**.

It is clear that the difference between having access to technology and not having it has an enormous impact on lifestyles. Technology offers many things, including security and quality of life.

> **Adjustment** involves taking actions to minimise the adverse impacts of a natural hazard.

Revision activity

Research ways in which technology is helping in the prediction of and adjustment to one natural hazard.

Now test yourself
Tested

5 What is environmental determinism?

Answer online

Unequal access
Revised

Although access to technology is strongly correlated with development (particularly wealth), there are other possible reasons for the lack of access:

● **physical** — renewable energy technology is of little interest to countries that lack the required sources of energy such as wind, water or solar power

● **environmental** — there are examples of new technologies being rejected on the grounds of possibly causing environmental damage, including growing GM crops and the application of pesticides

● **cost** — new technology is almost inevitably costly, so this immediately impedes access

● **corporate** — much of the research leading to advances in technology is undertaken by TNCs. They are often unwilling to share their innovations and are much more concerned with profit-making. The costs of research and development are extremely high and these costs need to be recouped. The laws of intellectual property and the patent system allow corporations to protect their innovations

● **political** — access to the internet is not available to the people of North Korea. It is not in the interests of its authoritarian government that the citizens should discover how poor their living conditions are compared with much of the rest of the world

● **military** — the Nuclear Non-proliferation Treaty aims to prevent the technology required to make nuclear weapons from falling into the hands of 'rogue' governments. The International Atomic Energy Agency tries to ensure that nuclear technology is used only for peaceful purposes such as the generation of electricity

● **religious** — the use of contraceptive technology is discouraged by some religions, most notably the Roman Catholic Church

● **moral** — we as individuals have our own views on technology. Some are uneasy about new technologies such as genetic engineering, IVF (*in vitro* fertilisation) or space exploration, so they opt not to take advantage of the technology

In addition to all the above reasons, we have to recognise that there are people in today's world who have no interest in modern technology and prefer to reject it — the **technophobes**.

Examiner's tip

Learn a range of examples of where and why technology is not available to some people.

Examiner's tip

Although access to technology is closely linked to development, be careful not to say that access is only about wealth and money.

Typical mistake

Candidates often claim that poverty is the reason for lack of access to technology, but that is not the whole story.

Revision activities

● Research the possible benefits and concerns about growing GM crops.
● Check that you understand what patents and intellectual property are.
● Find out how many countries (a) make peaceful use of nuclear power; (b) have nuclear weapons.

Now test yourself   Tested ▢

6   Why might politics act as a barrier to technology?
7   Why do some people reject modern technology? Give examples.

Answers online

Technology and development

The technology gap ——————————————————————— Revised ▢

There is a link between economic development and technological innovation. The developed world's advantage of being the first to industrialise is maintained by continual technological innovation.

The economies of the developed world are increasingly knowledge based; they have moved on from an industrial age to an information age. In a knowledge-based economy, money is made from ideas, information and services rather than goods. This progress has brought with it the infrastructure for still more technological advancement, namely:

● universities and research organisations, educating populations

● government-sponsored research and development

● TNCs keen to invest in new technologies and market them

● an advanced legal system that recognises and protects intellectual property and patents

● reliable water, energy, transport, health and communication systems

In short, new technology is one of the most important drivers of development. The growth of the knowledge-based economy has also been promoted by a number of factors, as shown in Figure 6.2

Figure 6.2 Factors promoting the growth of the knowledge-based economy

Although the developed world has entered an information age, much of the developing world is either just entering it or stuck in an industrial age. It is this that underlies the **technology gap**. Developing countries suffer a time lag between the development of new technology and their access to it.

Now test yourself   Tested ☐

8   What is a knowledge-based economy?
9   What is the technology gap?

Answers online

Technological leapfrogging   Revised ☐

The technology gap presents a challenge, particularly to emergent economies such as China and India which are impatient to become developed. Is there any way that they can avoid the time lag that is very much a feature of the technology gap? Is there a 'quick fix' or short-cut route? Is **technological leapfrogging** a possibility?

Technological leapfrogging occurs when a new technology is adopted without a precursor technology. A classic example is provided by the mobile phone, which is now used widely in countries that never had a network of landlines and telephone exchanges. The technologies that can leapfrog are characteristically mobile and physically small, such as laptops, WiFi and solar panels.

There is at least one major difficulty associated with technological leapfrogging, which is that most new technology involves huge expenditure on research and development by governments and TNCs. Understandably, there is a wish to recoup this money in full by means of royalties and profits, which means charging those people who need the technology but can least afford it.

Technological innovation costs

Most new technologies have particular aims but may have unforeseen impacts. A classic example is the Green Revolution, which was introduced in the 1960s. Its aim was to increase food production in developing countries. Although the objective was achieved in many places, there were undoubted costs:

● economic — farmers became dependent on high inputs of fertiliser, water and machinery, which were costly to buy

● social — societies became polarised between those farmers who could afford the high-yielding variety seeds, fertilisers and machinery and those who could not. The latter lost out and many became landless labourers

● environmental — the widespread use of agrochemicals led to eutrophication; overuse of irrigation caused salinisation of soils and water shortages; monoculture of HYVs of cereal led to them becoming prone to disease

The Gene Revolution is also beginning to reveal costs that need to be offset against some undoubted benefits.

> **Examiner's tip**
> Nuclear energy is a good example of the benefits and costs of new technology.

> **Typical mistake**
> There is a tendency to think, quite wrongly, that the plant breeding that was part of the Green Revolution is the same thing as the genetic modification of crops in the Gene Revolution.

> **Examiner's tip**
> It is important to show the examiner that you can take a balanced view of both the Green and Gene Revolutions.

> **Revision activity**
> Create a two-column table listing the costs and benefits of the Green Revolution.

The externalities of technology

Using technology has broader consequences or **externalities**. Broadly speaking, the positive economic and social externalities are known from the outset, but the negative environmental impacts of a heavy reliance on technology only subsequently become apparent:

● goods require resources, which are extracted from the environment and processed — both cause environmental damage

● manufacturing and urbanisation cause pollution

● most technology has to be powered or fuelled, which usually means burning fossil fuels — more carbon dioxide emissions lead to global warming

There are two approaches to this issue of environmental damage and pollution:

● **polluter pays** — the costs of pollution are calculated and passed on to the producer or user of the technology to pay

● **pollution sink** — it is assumed that the global environment provides a sink that is large enough to cope with all the atmospheric emissions and discharges of polluted water associated with the use of technology

It is unrealistic to hope that all pollution can be prevented. Therefore, in the case of carbon dioxide emissions, we should concentrate on reducing them by improving the efficiency with which fossil fuels are burnt and by capturing and storing pollutants before they enter the atmosphere.

> An **externality** is an impact — either a cost (negative) or a benefit (positive) — that is not accounted for in the initial economic costs of a product or process.

> **Revision activity**
> Find some examples of the application of the polluter pays principle.

Now test yourself Tested

11 Why is it that a heavy reliance on technology has negative externalities?
12 What is the difference between the 'polluter pays' and the 'pollution sink' approaches to the environment?

Answer online

Technology, environment and the future

Appropriate technology versus megaprojects Revised

This question frequently arises: what is the 'best' type of technology to use in a particular situation or to confront a particular problem? There are at least four approaches to answering this question (Table 6.1). They may be seen as located on two different axes, the one running from low-tech to high-tech and the other from labour-intensive to capital-intensive:

● Those who favour **intermediate technology** argue that technology needs to be low cost and easy to maintain and repair locally. In other words, the approach needs to be bottom-up with local people and organisations involved in the planning, building and maintenance. The technology needs to be fit for purpose.

● The **megaprojects** approach involves a top-down approach and the investment of huge amounts of capital and advanced technology. Almost inevitably, there are issues of maintenance and repair — bigger is rarely better.

● The **high-tech solutions** approach means there is a reliance on high-tech companies and a technological competence that at the moment have to come from the developed world.

● The **renewable future** approach means finding solutions that have the least environmental impact and cause the smallest amount of pollution. It might involve some sophisticated technology such as solar panels and wind turbines.

Examiner's tip

You are strongly advised to make use of examples from Topics 1 and 2 in this section.

Examiner's tip

There are many classes of technological fix (high-tech, intermediate, appropriate, renewable etc.). Make sure you learn definitions of each and have examples for all.

Table 6.1 Which kind of technological fix?

'Small is beautiful'	'The bigger the better'	'High-tech is best'	'Renewable future'
Intermediate technology — low cost, simple, small scale, using local skills and resources	Megaprojects that provide a one-off solution at very high capital cost	Most advanced solution currently available, e.g. nanotechnology, bioengineering and electronics	Alternative technology — lowest possible environmental impact and least pollution
Example: village hand pump installed by an NGO	Example: large dam funded by government	Example: nanofiltration systems from TNC research and development labs	Example: solar-powered water pump: TNC/NGO joint venture

Typical mistake

Candidates often wrongly cite projects like the Three Gorges dam in China as new technology. It is the technologies involved in the project that matter, not the project name.

Global environmental issues Revised

Most people are looking to technology to help overcome the worldwide environmental issues of global warming and land degradation. The sort of technological fixes required here are referred to as **planetary engineering** or **geo-engineering**.

'Fixing' desertification, a particularly acute form of land degradation, is a top priority particularly in China and sub-Saharan Africa. The strategies followed to date have not been geo-engineering in the true sense. They may be large scale, but they still rely on what is essentially intermediate technology, i.e. restricting livestock grazing, planting trees and conserving water.

Those in favour of geo-engineering argue that truly advanced techno-fixes (such as to check global warming by creating an artificial aerosol blanket in the atmosphere to reflect sunlight back into space) are more likely to work than persuading people and governments to change their lifestyles (an **attitudinal fix**) to reduce pollution. Opponents of geo-engineering, on the other hand, suggest that any solution would be essentially experimental with unknown outcomes.

An **attitudinal fix** is when people change their behaviour in order to reduce a problem rather than relying on new technology to solve the problem.

Typical mistake

Candidates often think that geo-engineering has already been undertaken to save the world from global warming.

Technology and sustainability Revised

Technology and environmental sustainability are not mutually exclusive. However, if the use of technology is to be made compatible with the concept of sustainability, some hard choices will have to be made (Figure 6.3). Is there a nation on Earth that is prepared to make the correct choices or will there be room for compromises?

Examiner's tip

Make sure you learn the definition of environmental sustainability for the exam and that you can apply it to different examples of technology to judge their sustainability. It is surprising how weak the understanding of sustainability really is.

- Technology must be cost effective and affordable, for instance not leading to debt
- Externalities must not pass costs on to others
- Technology should benefit all parts of society and not polarise it
- Technology should promote human health and wellbeing

- Technology should produce little pollution
- Technology must not have adverse consequences for ecosystems and biodiversity
- Technology should use renewable resources
- Power for technology should avoid fossil fuel use

Figure 6.3 Technology and sustainability

Technological futures

Revised ☐

The technological future of the world is by no means clear. There would seem to be three different future scenarios:

- A **divergent (technological-fixed versus technological-impoverished) world** with technological advances concentrated in the developed world and limited access to technology in the developing world. In effect, this is the status quo with a clearly defined technology gap.

- A **convergent (technology for all) world** involving a healthy transfer of technology from the developed to the developing world. This would gradually close the technology gap. The UN agencies and NGOs would have a major role to play in achieving this, with the cooperation of the TNCs.

- A **sustainable (renewable-reliant) world** with a major switch to renewable sources of energy to power technology. Such a switch would avoid the negative impacts of using oil, gas and coal and the economic uncertainties surrounding what happens when these resources eventually run out.

Revision activity

Find some examples of technology transfers that have worked.

Now test yourself

Tested ☐

17 What is the difference between a technologically convergent world and a divergent one?

18 How likely is it that the world will switch to renewable resources?

Answers online

Exam practice

Section A questions

1   The diagram below explores the idea that if a phone can do the job, who needs a PC?

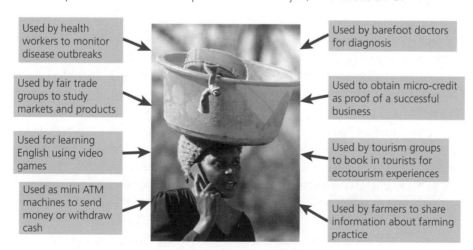

Used by health workers to monitor disease outbreaks

Used by fair trade groups to study markets and products

Used for learning English using video games

Used as mini ATM machines to send money or withdraw cash

Used by barefoot doctors for diagnosis

Used to obtain micro-credit as proof of a successful business

Used by tourism groups to book in tourists for ecotourism experiences

Used by farmers to share information about farming practice

(a) Using the diagram and your own knowledge, explain how mobile phones are revolutionising development in many low-income developing countries.   [10]

(b) Evaluate the reasons for inequality of access to advanced technology.   [15]

2 The diagram below shows the 'technological breakfast' as consumed by business people in the developed world.

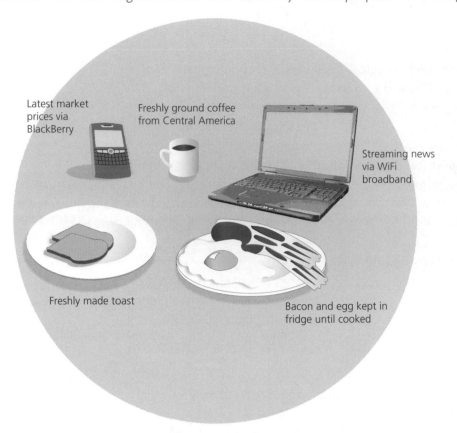

Latest market prices via BlackBerry

Freshly ground coffee from Central America

Streaming news via WiFi broadband

Freshly made toast

Bacon and egg kept in fridge until cooked

(a) Using examples, suggest why this technological breakfast is consumed in some countries but not others. **[10]**

(b) To what extent do different technological solutions to the same problem produce different impacts? **[15]**

Answers and quick quizzes online

Online

Examiner's summary

✔ There is a close link between technology and development. The beauty of technology is that it can do much to increase the ability of people to meet their demands for such things as food, manufactured goods, efficient transport, good communications, better health and security.

✔ Technology is not evenly distributed around the world. It is concentrated in the developed world where there is a high degree of dependence on it. Access to technology is also unevenly distributed, with much of the developing world technologically impoverished.

✔ There are many reasons for the restricted access to technology. Cost is a critical factor and governments and TNCs are key players. Some aspects of technology may be avoided for environmental, political, religious or moral reasons.

✔ At present the world is divided by a technology gap that separates the 'haves' (the developed world) from the 'have-nots' (the developing world). How to cross or close that gap is truly a global challenge.

✔ Although the intention of most technology is to do good, it is a sad fact that there is nearly always a downside of costs: economic, social and environmental. New technology also has wider impacts that only subsequently become apparent. These are the externalities and the negative ones are largely to do with the environment.

✔ There is an obvious and seemingly inescapable clash between technology and the environment. In this context, there are those who support the polluter pays principle as opposed to those who follow the pollution sink principle, i.e. that the environment has to cope with all that the human race throws at it.

- There is much debate as to what sort of technology constitutes the 'best' solution to a particular situation or problem. The term 'appropriate technology' is often heard in replies, but what that means exactly depends very much on the particular situation or problem.

- Geo-engineering has been suggested as offering solutions to some of the major environmental issues such as global warming and land degradation. To some, such solutions are little more than science fiction. To others, they threaten to be huge experiments with unknown outcomes. Still others argue that more is likely to be achieved by changing attitudes towards the environment and resources rather than by potentially dangerous macro-technology.

- The technological future is unclear, but it looks as if it will most likely be a continuation of the present divergent world with its technology gap. Attitudes will have to change if there is to be any significant technological convergence or a move to a more sustainable world.

7 Writing the report-style essay

Introducing Unit 4

How to succeed in Unit 4 Revised

In order to succeed in Unit 4, you need to understand how this unit differs from the other units that make up your geography A-level. The focus of this unit is the writing of a report-style essay to answer one question in a 1 hour and 30 minute exam.

The key to succeeding in Unit 4 is to collate a range of geographical information through research from a number of different sources such as books, geographical journals, videos and the internet in order to be able to write the report. Unit 4 will also build on your understanding of the work that you have completed throughout your A-level course.

The six option topics Revised

There are six options available to study and you must choose just one of them. You will be provided with a pre-released research focus detailing which aspect of the option you will be expected to write about in the exam, which is available about 4 weeks before the exam. The six options are:

● Option 1: Tectonic activity and hazards
● Option 2: Cold environments — landscapes and change
● Option 3: Life on the margins — the food supply problem
● Option 4: The world of cultural diversity
● Option 5: Pollution and human health at risk
● Option 6: Consuming the rural landscape — leisure and tourism

The options range from those with a strong focus on physical geography to those that are more concerned with social, environmental or cultural geography.

Introducing the mark scheme Revised

Whichever option topic you choose to answer, you will be assessed against a generic mark scheme for Unit 4 (Table 7.1). It assesses your ability to write a structured report-style essay that uses a range of suitable geographical examples, case studies and concepts to support a line of argument.

Answers and quick quizzes at **www.therevisionbutton.co.uk/myrevisionnotes**

Table 7.1 Generic mark scheme for Unit 4

Abbreviation	Component	Marks
D	Introducing, defining and focusing on the question	10
R	Research and methodology	15
A	Analysis, application and understanding	20
C	Conclusions and evaluation	15
Q	Quality of written expression and sourcing	10
Total		70

It is expected that the geographical content in candidates' answers may well be different, but all answers will be assessed against the DRACQ structure, which is broken down as follows:

- **D: Discuss/define** — how you introduce your report-style essay
- **R: Research and methodology** — the evidence and quality of your research
- **A: Application and understanding** — in response to the question set
- **C: Conclusions and evaluation** — how you conclude your report-style essay and evaluate the value of the evidence you have put forward
- **Q: Quality of written communication** — how you structure your report and the quality of your communication skills in answering the question

Geographical research

Researching the issues   Revised ☐

It is important that you develop the required research skills needed for this exam so that you can research a range of material and develop the cases studies and examples that will support your answer in the exam. Make sure you are clear about *what* you are researching and *how* you will record the information that you have collected (pages 73–78).

For example, as part of Option 2: Cold environments, you will need to research 'cold environments in which humans are attempting to take the opportunities available by overcoming the challenges'. This statement from the specification gives you a clear research focus. Take these statements and begin your research, extending the work you have carried out in class. A good starting point is to decide on a particular location that you wish to focus on. In this case, Alaska in the USA would fit well, enabling you to start exploring the ways in which people are using technology to overcome the challenges of Alaska's extreme environment.

Using fieldwork   Revised ☐

Each option topic offers you the opportunity to do some first-hand fieldwork in order to provide a wider range of material for the exam. You may have had the opportunity to develop some fieldwork as part of your class work but, if not, put aside some time for this. As part of the A-level specification (available at **www.edexcel.com**) there is a clear steer towards developing fieldwork for Unit 4. For example, as part of Option

3: Life on the margins — the food supply problem, there is a suggestion that you could visit contrasting local farms including organic holdings and those taking part in LEAF (Linking Environment and Farming) schemes. You would need to record details of the farm type and the methods used and this could then form part of the evidence you use in the exam.

Examiner's tip

Many candidates overlook fieldwork but it can be a good way of showing the examiner that you have carried out a wide range of data collection and a good way of scoring highly in the R and A components.

Command words
Revised

There are a number of key command words that are used in the exam (Table 7.2). You need to know how to respond to these and how to use the research that you have carried out in order to support a line of argument that you will develop in your report-style essay. All of these command words are intended to encourage you to analyse a range of points of view and use evidence to support the view that you think is the most important.

Table 7.2 Key command words

Word	Response
Assess	Weigh up both sides of an issue/solution and come to a conclusion
Discuss	Give both sides of an argument (for and against) and come to a conclusion
Evaluate	Weigh up several options or arguments and come to a conclusion about their importance/success
Explain	Provide a detailed set of reasons to say why something is like it is
To what extent	Say 'how far' you agree with a statement or option by examining its advantages and disadvantages

(D) Describing, defining and discussing the issue

How to achieve top marks
Revised

In order to achieve top marks, you must write a clear introduction to your report-style essay in which you give:

● a focus to your report-style essay, clearly identifying the issue that you are going to be writing about and setting out the background so that the examiner knows that you understand the issue

● a framework of how you will be going about tackling the question that you have been set in the exam. You need to clearly give the examiner a structure that you will be using in order to answer the question set. Make sure you justify the use of any examples and case studies that you will include in your report

● definitions of the key words that you will be using, taken from the question title — note that many of the key words you need to know are defined or given in bold in the six option topics in this book

By closely following these guidelines in the exam, you can hit the top box for marks in this section. It means being clear what you are writing about, what the key words are and how you will tackle the question.

Table 7.3 Mark scheme for component D

Marks	Describing, defining and discussing the issue
9–10	Clear reference to the title; develops a focus
	Indication of framework, either by concepts and/or case studies
	Accurate definitions of key terms
6–8	Some framework/focus, either by concepts and/or case studies
	Incomplete definitions of key terms
3–5	Some reference to the title
	Some definitions of key terms and/or some framework
1–2	Limited introduction
	Vague definitions of key terms and/or framework
0	No attempt to introduce the report

> **Examiner's tip**
>
> Some candidates use three separate sub-headings in their introduction: focus, framework and definitions. Better candidates in the exam *justify* why they have selected their focus and why they have selected their framework.

> **Examiner's tip**
>
> Make sure your introduction is specific to the exam question on the day and not a 'prepared' introduction, which are usually too generalised and score low marks.

> **Typical mistake**
>
> Many candidates rush this part of their report-style essay as they want to launch into their case study evidence. Take your time to ensure that this section receives the attention that it deserves.

(R) Researching the issue

How to achieve top marks

Revised

In order to succeed in achieving top marks in this section, you need to show the examiner evidence:

- of a wide range of carefully selected research that is applicable to the question set
- that you understand the background theory that underpins the ideas and themes you are writing about — make sure you include any models or theories
- of how you selected the research material that you will be using as evidence to support your line of argument in your report-style essay

Table 7.4 Mark scheme for component R

Marks	Researching the issue
12–15	Wide range of relevant case studies used (by scale and/or location)
	Relevant concepts and/or theories used
	Factual, accurate, topical evidence
	Indication of methodology, i.e. how evidence was sampled/selected from a range of resources available
8–11	A range (scale/location) of all/mostly relevant case studies used
	Some evidence of concepts and/or theories
	Mostly accurate data
	Some indication of methodology, i.e. how evidence was sampled/selected from a range of resources available
5–7	Some range of case studies/concepts, but lacks selection
	May have inaccuracies in factual/conceptual data
	Lacks methodology/sourcing
1–4	Basic research
	Limited case study material/concepts or lacks relevance or selection
0	Case studies/concepts missing and no evidence of research

Sourcing your research

As you start to research, it is important that you keep a list of all the sources that you read and use. You can include some of these in your report to show the examiner that you have carried out a range of research and this will contribute to the mark that you achieve in this section of the mark scheme. You should always provide the title, date and author of your sources, but you may wish to go further by using the Harvard or author-date system of referencing. This involves stating:

● the author(s)
● the date the book was published in brackets
● the title of the book in italics
● where the book was published
● the publisher

For example:

Cloke, P., Crang, P. and Goodwin, M. (eds) (2005) *Introducing Human Geographies* (2nd edition). London: Arnold.

One of the most common ways of researching is by using the internet. This also requires clear sourcing and the date you accessed the information. For example:

Arctic ice melt 'like adding 20 years of CO_2 emissions' (2012). Available at www.bbc.co.uk/news/science-environment-19496674 (accessed: 6 September 2012).

By compiling a list of all the research you have carried out, you will be able to walk confidently into the exam and name some of the sources that you have used in your methodology (see below).

> **Examiner's tip**
>
> You do not need to remember all the sources that you have researched in the exam. However, it is good practice to be able to state a range of them throughout your report and to produce a list of several key sources.

> **Typical mistake**
>
> Don't reference research by saying 'a geography textbook' or 'the one with the blue front cover' — this does not demonstrate that you have carried out proper research.

Producing a methodology

You should include a methodology in your answer. This can be done either by writing a methodology paragraph or by including a methodology table. Your methodology can also be used to evaluate the reliability and the topicality of the sources that you have used. Your methodology can be included in your report-style essay in several different ways:

● as an ongoing methodology throughout your report-style essay
● following on from your introduction as part of setting your framework and focus
● at the end of your report

If you use a table format, it could be presented as follows, although other headings could also be used.

Area of focus	Source material	Evaluation of source

> **Examiner's tip**
>
> You may find it helpful to produce this table at the end of your report as soon as the exam starts, so that you can add to it throughout the exam as you include information that you have researched. All pages of your exam booklet will be seen by the examiner, so don't worry if it's at the back.

Make sure you identify how reliable your sources are. More reliable information will have been published by academic institutions or been peer reviewed. Less reliable information may have been sponsored or posted anonymously on the internet. Be careful about using any information from Wikipedia or YouTube, for example — check carefully that it is not biased.

(A) Analysing the issue

How to achieve top marks
Revised ☐

In order to achieve top marks in this section, you need to demonstrate that you have:

- selected appropriate case study material in order to tackle the question that has been set. Make sure you understand what is being asked of you and that you have a clear focus and framework in your introduction, which will help you select which case studies to use to develop your answer

- shown that you understand what the question is asking and that you develop a clear line of argument to support a given viewpoint. If you are asked to discuss an issue, make sure you balance the arguments for and against, even if you ultimately decide to take one viewpoint in your conclusion. A cogent argument is one that is persuasive and conclusive and uses evidence to support it

- shown that you understand that different people have different opinions about the issue you are writing about. It is important that you have the ability to appreciate these different viewpoints, even if you do not agree with them

- included any maps and diagrams that will support your line of argument and answer in general

Table 7.5 Mark scheme for component A

Marks	Analysing the issue
17–20	All research applied directly to the question set
	High conceptual understanding and cogent argument
	Appreciation of different values/perspectives about the question
	Any maps/diagrams are used to support the answer
13–16	Most of the research is used to support the question
	Some conceptual understanding
	Some appreciation of values/perspectives
	Any maps/diagrams are usually used to support the answer
9–12	Generalised material
	Simple explanations
	Limited appreciation of values/perspectives
	Any maps/diagrams are sometimes used to support the answer
1–8	Descriptive, with very limited appreciation of values/perspectives
	Any maps/diagrams are rarely used to support the answer
0	Descriptive report lacking in detail; lacks application to the question

Selecting your case studies

It is important that you select carefully which case study material you wish to include in your answer. You may find that you do not need to include *all* of the research that you have carried out for a particular example or case study — be selective. Some of your case study material may only get used in passing reference to help build up a line of argument, but some research will need to be explained fully and in detail as a key part of your answer.

You may find it helpful to develop a range of case studies that you can learn before you go into the exam so that you can select the appropriate case studies for your answer. You can do this by completing case study information sheets similar to the one given in Figure 7.1.

> **Examiner's tip**
>
> The best candidates include accurate, selective case study and example material that is relevant to the question asked.

Title of case study:
References used:
Level of development: MEDC/NIC/LEDC/LDC
Location of case study:
Relationship to issue:
Issues covered in case study (socio-economic, environmental, political):
Reliability of resources used:

Figure 7.1 Sample case study information sheet

Maps and diagrams

Appropriate maps and diagrams can be included — perhaps two or three. You need to think carefully about whether using them will enhance your line of argument or support the case study that you have chosen to use. Be sure that the map or diagram:

- says something that adds to what that you have written rather than replicating what you have already said
- explains something that is easier as a diagram, perhaps a model or theory
- is annotated — a clear location map with annotated information of, for example, a number of tectonic events around the Pacific ring of fire will enable you to convey a large amount of information in a short space of time

> **Examiner's tip**
>
> Don't include maps that just show the location of a place you have written about. These are a waste of time and will not help you to develop an answer.

> **Typical mistake**
>
> Many candidates launch into the main body of their report-style essay by writing all that they can remember about the case studies that they have learnt. This detracts from any line of argument that is being built up. Be selective and apply information to the question.

(C) Concluding and evaluating the issue

How to achieve top marks — Revised

In order to achieve the top marks in this section, you need to include a clear conclusion to your report and evaluate the strength of this conclusion. This can be done by:

- clearly stating the conclusion at the end of your report and labelling it clearly and appropriately
- summarising the main thrust of your argument throughout your report and briefly citing the case studies (evidence) that support this line of argument
- evaluating the evidence that you use as you include it in your report. This may involve you writing short (mini) sub-conclusions when you have used evidence to support a point that you have made
- evaluating the strength of your conclusion by showing the examiner that there is evidence to support the view that you have taken
- pointing out any anomalies, i.e. evidence that does not fit the argument
- showing the examiner that you understand that the question you have been set is complex and that a range of different viewpoints may exist. It is fine for you to accept that there may not be a simple answer to the question set and that you may not be able to come to a clear decision about what you think the answer is, as long as you can justify why you are saying this and use your case study material as evidence
- making sure you have a clear conclusion section in your report that refers back to the question you have been asked to answer. Summarise the key points of your argument, refer back to any models or theories that you have used and review the evidence that you put forward

Table 7.6 Mark scheme for component C

Marks	Concluding and evaluating the issue
12–15	Clearly stated
	Thorough recall of content/case studies used in report
	Ongoing evaluation throughout report
	Understands the complexity of the question
8–11	Meaningful, based on content of report
	Selective recall of content of report
	Some evaluation, either ongoing or in final conclusion
5–7	Vague conclusion, related tenuously to report
	Very limited evaluations
1–4	An attempt at an evaluation of the question even if no end conclusion
0	No conclusion or evaluation within report

Typical mistake

Many candidates don't allow enough time in the exam to write a thorough conclusion. Make sure you give yourself plenty of time — remember, there are more marks available for this section than for the introduction.

Examiner's tip

Make sure you include ongoing evaluation in your report by summarising each case study or theme and stating how its inclusion supports the answer you are writing.

(Q) Quality of written communication

How to achieve top marks

There are a number of key things you have to do to score highly in this part of the mark scheme. In order to achieve top marks in this section, you need to demonstrate that you have:

● a clear structure to your report-style essay, with clear headings and sub-sections. Planning your answer in your exam booklet at the start will enable you to do this more effectively

● written clearly in order to demonstrate high standards of spelling and punctuation. Many candidates do not take the time in the exam to ensure this is done properly

● learnt the proper geographical vocabulary for the option that you are writing about

● included appropriate maps or diagrams and that you have incorporated them into your text appropriately, with clear captions and labels — take the time to do this

● referenced the source material that you have included in your answer. You also need to demonstrate that you have researched a wide range of information from a number of different sources

> **Examiner's tip**
> Plan your work to ensure that you write a clear report-style essay with headings and sub-headings throughout your answer.

Table 7.7 Mark scheme for component Q

Marks	Quality of written communication
9–10	Coherent structure and sequencing, with obvious report-style sub-sections
	Excellent standards of spelling and punctuation
	Geographical vocabulary used correctly
	Diagrams and maps, if used, incorporated into text and support argument
	Referenced/acknowledged material; obvious evidencing/sourcing from a wide range of sources (texts, journals, internet, DVDs etc.)
6–8	Generally clearly written with some report-style sub-sections
	Some organisation and sequencing
	Good standard of punctuation and spelling
	Some good use of appropriate geographical vocabulary
	May have diagrammatic/cartographic use but not always incorporated into text
	Referenced/acknowledged material; occasional evidencing/sourcing from a wide range of sources (texts, journals, internet, DVDs etc.)
3–5	Basic syntax, some errors of punctuation and spelling
	Disjointed organisation and sequencing, although may have some sub-sections
	Some errors in punctuation and spelling
	Some use of appropriate geographical vocabulary
	May have diagrammatic/cartographic use but rarely incorporated into text
	Referenced/acknowledged material; rare evidencing/sourcing from a wide range of sources (texts, journals, internet, DVDs etc.)
1–2	Very basic quality of written communication
	Frequent spelling and punctuation errors
	Low level syntax
	Occasional use of geographical vocabulary
	Referenced/acknowledged material; lacks evidencing/sourcing from a wide range of sources (texts, journals, internet, DVDs etc.)
0	Basic standards of quality of written communication not met

Preparing for the exam

The pre-released research focus

Revised ▢

About 4 weeks before the exam, you will be given a pre-released research focus that will 'steer' you towards which parts of the option you need to prepare in detail. This pre-release is made up of two sections:

- explore — in which you are guided towards the enquiry question(s) or parts of enquiry questions that will be the focus of the exam. This includes understanding the background concepts and theories of the option unit
- research — which suggests the supporting case study and example material that you will need to have researched in order to support your answer. It often refers to scale and sometimes to levels of development

Examiner's tip

Be careful not to be too narrow in your focus of case study material in preparation — the best answers usually show an appreciation of all aspects of the option.

Examiner's summary

Remember that when you write your answer in the exam, you keep the five components of the mark scheme in focus:

- ✔ (D) Describing, defining and discussing the issue — write a clear introduction, which has a focus, a framework and definitions of the key geographical terminology.
- ✔ (R) Researching the issue — ensure that you include a wide range of relevant research that can be used as evidence to support a clear line of argument and that you understand the background theory to your chosen option.
- ✔ (A) Analysing the issue — demonstrate that you have selected appropriate case study and example material and that you understand what the question is asking you. Develop a balanced answer that shows the

examiner that you understand that there is a range of views about the issue you are writing about and include appropriate maps and diagrams.

- ✔ (C) Concluding and evaluating the issue — clearly state a conclusion at the end of the report and summarise the key arguments that you have made in your report. Evaluate the evidence you have put forward and demonstrate to the examiner that you understand the complexity of the question you have been set.
- ✔ (Q) Quality of written communication — ensure that you have clear headings in your answer, with high standards of punctuation and grammar and that you can spell key geographical terms correctly. Reference your material appropriately by completing a methodology table.

8 Tectonic activity and hazards

Tectonic hazards and causes

Tectonic activity
Revised

A **tectonic event** is the result of a movement or deformation of the Earth's crust. Tectonic events are usually earthquakes or volcanic eruptions.

A **tectonic hazard** is when a tectonic event has the potential to have an impact on people resulting in loss of life and/or physical damage to property. Not all tectonic events are hazardous as many earthquakes occur deep below the Earth's surface, are low in magnitude or occur far from where people are living.

A **tectonic disaster** is when a tectonic event occurs and causes extensive loss of life, damage and destruction. The Haiti earthquake in 2010 was a magnitude 7.0 earthquake with its epicentre 25 km west of the capital city Port-au-Prince. It caused 316 000 deaths, making it one of the deadliest earthquakes of all time.

> **Now test yourself** — Tested
>
> 1 Explain the difference between a tectonic hazard and a tectonic disaster.
>
> **Answer online**

> **Examiner's tip**
>
> Tectonic activity and hazards is one of the most popular options studied as part of Unit 4. You need to make sure your report is factually correct and well structured in order to stand out.

> **Examiner's tip**
>
> Make sure you learn the facts and figures for a range of up-to-date (within the last 10 years) examples of tectonic hazards and disasters.

> **Examiner's tip**
>
> You can use older case studies, but there needs to be a good justification for this such as the lack of a more recent event of that type or an unusual event.

> **Revision activity**
>
> Explain what tectonic hazards are and what causes them.

Event profile of hazards
Revised

Tectonic hazards can vary greatly in their profile. This means that they can differ in how often they occur, how powerful they are, how long they last and how much area (land) they affect. A hazard event profile is a diagram that represents the key characteristics of different types of tectonic hazards (Figure 8.1).

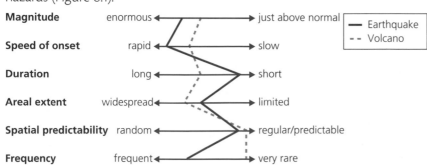

Figure 8.1 A typical hazard event profile for an earthquake (destructive boundary) and a volcano

> **Now test yourself**
>
> 2 Describe the event profile of an earthquake and a volcano.
>
> **Answer online**
>
> Tested

The causes of tectonic hazards

Revised

The Earth's surface is made up of a number of large plates that are in constant motion, moving very slowly. Ocean floors are continually moving, spreading from the centre and sinking at the edges. These tectonic plates slide on the mantle (made up of hot partially molten rock), which is deep beneath the Earth's crust (Figure 8.2).

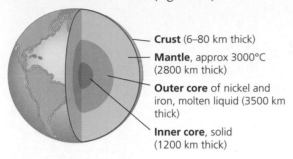

Crust (6–80 km thick)

Mantle, approx 3000°C (2800 km thick)

Outer core of nickel and iron, molten liquid (3500 km thick)

Inner core, solid (1200 km thick)

Figure 8.2 The structure of the Earth

Convection currents in the mantle move the plates. Convection currents are circular movements of the mantle material that rise from the core and cool as they meet the crust before falling again to return to the core to be heated once more. It is at the edges of the tectonic plates — the plate boundaries — where earthquakes and volcanoes occur most often because of weaknesses or faults where the plates meet (Figure 8.3).

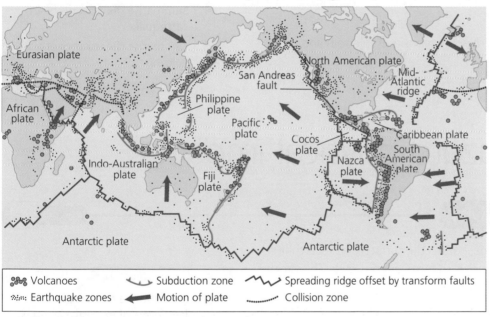

Eurasian plate

North American plate

San Andreas fault

Mid-Atlantic ridge

Philippine plate

Pacific plate

African plate

Cocos plate

Caribbean plate

Nazca plate

South American plate

Indo-Australian plate

Fiji plate

Antarctic plate

Antarctic plate

🌋 Volcanoes   ⌣ Subduction zone   ⋀⋁ Spreading ridge offset by transform faults

⋯ Earthquake zones   ← Motion of plate   ⋯⋯ Collision zone

> **Examiner's tip**
>
> You need to know the structure of the Earth and the location of the major tectonic plates and plate boundaries.

Figure 8.3 Global distribution of earthquakes and volcanoes

Different types of plate margins

Revised

Four types of plate boundary can be found where the plates meet:

- **destructive plate margin**, where one plate sinks beneath another (subduction) as they collide. The upper plate crumples, creating new mountains and volcanoes
- **constructive plate margin**, where two plates are moving apart from each other. Molten rock from the mantle rises to the surface, cools and hardens, forming a ridge of new rock. Volcanic eruptions are common

- **conservative plate margin**, where two plates are sliding past each other. Pressure builds up until they move with a jerk, causing earthquakes
- **collision plate margin**, where two continental plates collide and are crushed against each other. They are pushed upwards to form new mountains

Earthquakes occur when rocks within the Earth suddenly break or shift under stress, sending shock waves rippling:

- earthquake waves are measured on sensitive instruments called **seismographs**
- the **Richter scale** (and the more modern Moment Magnitude scale) assigns earthquakes a number based on the energy of its seismic waves
- thousands of earthquakes occur every day around the globe, although most of them are too weak to be felt
- every year about 10 000 people on average die as a result of earthquakes

Volcanoes are vents in the Earth's surface from which molten rock, debris and steam erupt:

- an eruption begins when magma, the molten rock from deep in the Earth's crust, rises toward the surface
- although some volcanoes are considered extinct, many are capable of rumbling to life again
- volcanoes provide valuable mineral deposits, fertile soils and geothermal energy
- about 1900 volcanoes are active today or are known to have been active in historical times

Now test yourself

3 Create a table contrasting the features and hazards at the four types of plate boundary.

4 Summarise the features of an earthquake.

5 Summarise the features of a volcano.

Answers online

Tested ☐

Tectonic hazard physical impacts

Extrusive igneous activity ———— Revised ☐

Once magma flows out (extrudes) on to the surface of the Earth it is referred to as lava, which then cools to form igneous rock. This process creates a number of significant landforms:

- **volcanic cones** — cone-shaped volcanoes that are formed from the build-up of lava on the surface of the Earth
- **fissures** — vents on a volcano through which lava can erupt
- **lava plateaux** — flat, extensive lava fields produced by volcanic activity

Now test yourself

6 Describe the three main landforms of extrusive igneous activity.

Answer online

Tested ☐

Different types of volcano ———— Revised ☐

Volcanoes can generally be grouped into four main types:

- **Cinder cones** are volcanoes built from ejected lava from a single vent. As the lava is blown violently into the air, it breaks into small fragments that solidify around the vent to form a cone. Most cinder cones tend to have a bowl-shaped crater at the summit and do not rise above 300 m in height, e.g. Mt Gordon in Alaska.

- **Composite volcanoes** (stratovolcanoes) are typically steep-sided, symmetrical cones built from layers of lava flows, volcanic ash, cinders and bombs. Most composite volcanoes have a crater at the summit, which can contain a central vent or a group of vents. These can rise up to as high as 2.4 km, e.g. Mt Pinatubo in the Philippines.
- **Shield volcanoes** are typically dome-shaped with gentle sides and a wide base. They are built up slowly over time from numerous basaltic lava flows. These volcanoes can stretch for up to 6.5 km and can reach 300 m in height, e.g. Mauna Loa on Hawaii.
- **Lava domes** are more typically dome-shaped with steep sides and a narrow base. They are formed as viscous lava flows slowly and therefore cools on the sides of the dome, expanding it further, e.g. Soufrière Hills on Montserrat.

Now test yourself

7 Describe each of the four main types of volcano and give an example of each.

Answer online

Tested

Intrusive igneous activity

Revised

Intrusive igneous activity is when magma cools and solidifies within the Earth's crust. This can lead to the formation of the following landforms after weathering and erosion has exposed them at the surface:

- **batholith** — a large emplacement of rock that forms from cooled magma deep in the Earth's crust, e.g. the Half Dome in Yosemite National Park, USA
- **laccolith** — magma is forced between two layers of sedimentary rock, creating a dome-shaped feature, e.g. Devil's Tower in Wyoming, USA
- **sill** — magma has intruded between layers of sedimentary rock, e.g. the Whin Sill in Northumberland
- **dike** — magma has cut discordantly across massive rock formations, e.g. Mackenzie dike swarm in the Northwest Territories, Canada

Now test yourself

8 Describe the landforms that can arise from intrusive igneous activity.

Answer online

Tested

Effects of earthquakes on landscapes

Revised

Earthquakes have less dramatic impacts on the landscape of the Earth:

- **rift valleys** can form where two oceanic plates are diverging, such as the mid-Atlantic ridge, or where continental crust is being stretched by divergence, such as in the East African Rift valley
- **fault scarps** are cliff-like features that can range from a few metres to hundreds of metres in height and can be several hundred kilometres long. They also form where two plates are diverging

Revision activity

Describe the impacts that tectonic activity can have on landscapes.

Now test yourself

Tested

9 What effects can earthquakes have on landscapes?

Answer online

Tectonic hazard human impacts

Why do people live in tectonically active areas?

Despite the evident risks, many people choose to live in tectonically active areas. This is because of a number of reasons:

- **lack of knowledge** — the long gap between some tectonic events means communities slowly forget that the area is at risk
- **lack of choice** — some people remain living in tectonically active areas because they lack the choice or there are few alternatives. This may be especially true for very poor people who may rely on the quality of land for subsistence farming
- **inertia** — there may be traditional, historical or cultural reasons for living close to volcanoes and this may prevent people from moving away

> **Now test yourself**
>
> 10 Explain three reasons why people may choose to live in tectonically active areas.
>
> **Answer online**
>
> Tested

Economic and social impacts

Tectonic hazards can have a range of economic and social impacts, as shown in Table 8.1.

Table 8.1 Economic and social impacts of tectonic hazards

Economic	Social
• Cost of repairing damage	• Cost to people in terms of casualties and loss of life
• Cost of rebuilding	• Misery, suffering and poor health
• Indirect costs of loss of earnings, loss of tourism income etc.	• Loss of infrastructure — damage to roads, services, electricity, water etc.
• Cost of emergency operations	

> **Now test yourself**
>
> 11 Explain some of the economic and social impacts of tectonic hazards.
>
> **Answer online**
>
> Tested

Specific impacts

You need to know the impacts that tectonic hazards can have on a range of specific locations around the world in countries at different stages of development. A selection of good examples to research further is included in Table 8.2.

Table 8.2 Examples of tectonic hazards for further research

Earthquakes	Volcanic eruptions
2011 Tōhoku, Japan	Ongoing Soufrière Hills, Montserrat
2010 Haiti	2010 Eyjafjallajökull, Iceland
2008 Sichuan, China	2007 Etna, Sicily, Italy

> **Examiner's tip**
>
> You may well have studied a number of different case studies and examples as part of your research preparation for this exam. It is best that you stick with the ones that you know well and have already researched in detail.

> **Now test yourself**
>
> Tested
>
> 12 Produce two detailed case studies highlighting the impacts of an earthquake in a less developed country and the impacts in a more developed country.
>
> **Answer online**

> **Revision activity**
>
> Outline the impacts that tectonic activities can have on people.

Trends in frequency and impact over time

Revised

Tectonic hazards can have varying patterns of impact over time, as shown by Park's response model (Figure 8.4). Different hazard events can have different impacts. This is shown by the speed of the drop in quality of life, the duration of the decline and the speed and nature of recovery. The differences in the three lines could be related to the type of hazard, the degree of preparedness or the speed of the relief effort and the nature of recovery and rebuilding.

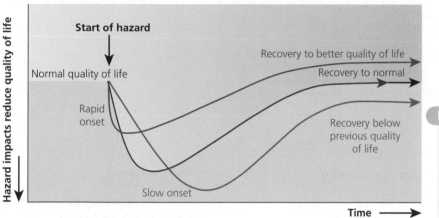

Figure 8.4 Park's response model

Now test yourself

13 Explain how Park's model shows that tectonic hazards can have different impacts over time.

Answer online

Tested

Response to tectonic hazards

Varying approaches

Revised

A range of approaches exist in attempting to cope with tectonic hazards:

● **do nothing** — people accept that tectonic activity is part of a daily routine in life and live with the outcomes whatever they may be

● **adjust** — people alter their lives or routines to factor in the risk that tectonic activity could impact on them. For example, individuals in San Francisco may ensure that furniture in their apartments is secured to walls to prevent it falling in the case of an earthquake or the government in Japan organises events to prepare the population for an earthquake event

● **leave** — people who may have already suffered the disastrous impacts of a tectonic event decide that their only option is to move away from the area to avoid suffering the long-term consequences or for fear of a repeat event

The response that people adopt may well be dependent on their personal experience of a tectonic hazard, but this may be influenced by their economic situation or the economic situation of their country.

Now test yourself

14 Explain the range of different approaches that exist to coping with tectonic hazards.

Answer online

Tested

Strategies involved in adjustment

Revised

The ways in which people attempt to cope vary before, during and after the tectonic event, as shown in Figure 8.5.

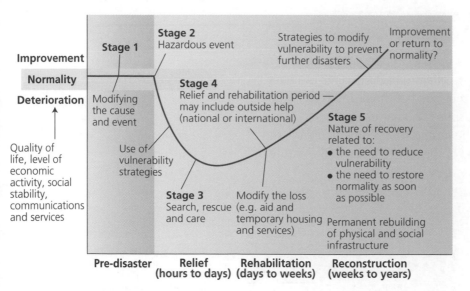

Figure 8.5 A disaster–response curve

15 Summarise the ways in which people attempt to cope before, during and after a tectonic hazard.

Answer online

Revision activity

Explain some of the ways in which people cope with tectonic hazards.

The effectiveness of different approaches   Revised ☐

Strategies for coping with tectonic hazards may also change and develop over time, as shown in Figure 8.6.

Modify the loss	Modify vulnerability	Modify the event	Modify the cause
• Aid vital for poor people • Insurance more useful for people in richer communities and countries	• Prediction and warning • Community preparedness • Education to change behaviour and prevent hazards realising into disasters	• Further environmental control • Hazard avoidance by land-use zoning • Hazard-resistant design (e.g. building design to resist earthquakes) • Engineering defences useful for coastal and river floods • Retro fitting of homes is possible for protection	• Environmental control • Hazard prevention • Only really possible for small-scale hazards, landslides/ avalanches and floods

Increasingly technological →

Figure 8.6 Response analysis framework

16 Explain how strategies for coping with tectonic hazards may change over time.

Answer online

Exam practice

Report-style essay

'The frequency of tectonic hazards and disasters has changed over time'. Discuss. [70]

Pre-released research focus

● Explore the trends and frequencies of tectonic hazards and disasters.

● Research a range of tectonic events and whether their risk has altered over time.

Answers and quick quizzes online

Online

Examiner's summary

✔ There are tectonic events, hazards and disasters.

✔ Tectonic hazards can vary greatly in how often they occur, how powerful they are, how long they last and how much area they affect.

✔ The Earth's surface is made up of a number of large plates that are in constant motion.

✔ There are four types of plate boundaries that can be found where the plates meet.

✔ Magma that extrudes on to the surface of the Earth cools to form igneous rock which creates a number of significant landforms.

✔ Volcanoes can generally be grouped into four main types: cinder cones, composite volcanoes, shield volcanoes and lava domes.

✔ Intrusive igneous activity is when magma cools and solidifies within the Earth's crust.

✔ Earthquakes have less dramatic impacts on the landscape of the Earth.

✔ Many people choose to live in tectonically active areas due to a number of reasons.

✔ Tectonic hazards can have a range of economic and social impacts.

✔ Tectonic hazards have different impacts in different locations around the world.

✔ Tectonic hazards can have varying patterns of impact over time.

✔ There is a range of approaches that exist in attempting to cope with tectonic hazards.

✔ The ways in which people attempt to cope with tectonic hazards vary before, during and after the tectonic event.

✔ Strategies for coping with tectonic hazards change and develop over time.

Defining and locating cold environments

Cold, glacial and periglacial environments

A cold environment is an area on the Earth's surface that experiences a significant period of time when the temperature is close to or below 0°C. There are four main types of cold environments:

- **polar** — high-latitude cold environments where temperatures can fall as low as –50°C in winter. Examples are Antarctica, Greenland and within the Arctic circle

- **alpine** — mountain areas where the high altitude means that temperatures are much colder than at sea level. Temperatures can fall as low as –10°C in winter. Examples are the Alps and the Rocky Mountains

- **glacial** — environments that are located around glaciers and found high up in alpine mountain ranges

- **periglacial** — located on the fringes of polar or glacial environments and will have permanently frozen ground (permafrost). Examples include parts of Canada, Greenland and Siberia

Examiner's tip

Make sure you are familiar with the key environments for this unit and that you can clearly distinguish between them and locate them in the world.

Revision activity

Explain what cold environments are and describe where they can be found.

Now test yourself

1 Summarise the four types of cold environment.

Answer online

Tested

Concepts of cold landscape systems

Revised

A cold landscape system may be understood through a systems approach (Figure 9.1).

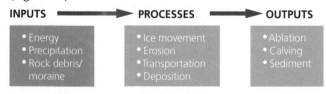

INPUTS ➡ PROCESSES ➡ OUTPUTS

INPUTS	PROCESSES	OUTPUTS
• Energy • Precipitation • Rock debris/moraine	• Ice movement • Erosion • Transportation • Deposition	• Ablation • Calving • Sediment

Figure 9.1 Inputs, processes and outputs

The **glacial system** is made up of two zones, as shown in Figure 9.2. The **accumulation zone** is where there is a gain in the amount of ice over the course of a year: inputs exceed outputs. The **ablation zone** is where there is a loss in the amount of ice over the course of a year: outputs exceed inputs. The equilibrium line is the boundary where gains and losses are balanced. The **mass balance** is the balance between the inputs and outputs of snow and ice and can be positive or negative.

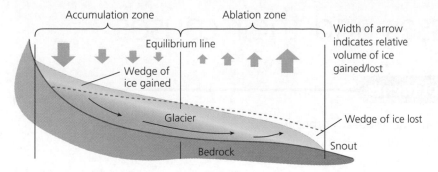

Figure 9.2 The glacial system

Frequency refers to how often an event happens, whereas **magnitude** refers to the size of an event. **Equifinality** refers to the fact that in an open system such as a glacial system the same end result can be reached by many different means. **Dynamic equilibrium** is the way in which the glacial system produces a dynamic response to balance any disturbance that may occur.

Now test yourself

2   Draw an annotated sketch of the glacial system.

Answer online

Tested

Revised

Different cold environments

Cold landscapes were more extensive in the past than they are today. There have been repeated glacial periods interspersed by warmer interglacial periods (Figure 9.3). The last glacial period occurred between 110 000 and 10 000 years ago and in Britain is called the Devensian glaciation.

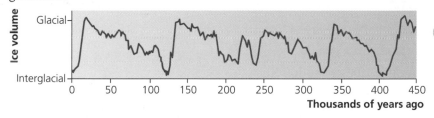

Figure 9.3 Glacial and interglacial periods of the last half a million years

Now test yourself

3   How have cold environments changed throughout the Earth's history?

Answer online

Tested

Past and present-day distribution

Revised

Britain has experienced much colder environments than it does today. In the past, glacial environments were found in Scotland, the Lake District, North Wales and parts of Ireland. Figure 9.4 shows the extent of the glacial environments over the last 2 million years of the Quaternary period in Britain.

Now test yourself   Tested

4   Describe the extent of the glacial environments of the Quaternary period in Britain.

Answer online

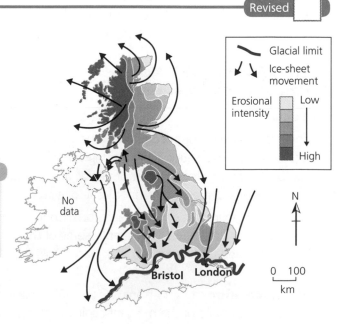

Figure 9.4 The glacial maximum in Britain

9 Cold environments — landscape and change

Climatic processes and their causes

Climatic causes of cold environments

Revised

The climatic causes of cold environments include global atmospheric circulation, polar anticyclones and the influence of latitude and altitude upon climate.

Global atmospheric circulation is the large-scale movement of air, which distributes thermal energy on the surface of the Earth. This circulation of air creates polar cells in which cold dense air tends to sink, leading to cold dry environments at the North and South poles.

Polar anticyclones are high pressure areas that form over the poles during the winter months as a result of the polar cells, e.g. the Siberian anticyclone.

In terms of the **influence of latitude and altitude upon climate**, in high latitude areas the sun is low in the sky and therefore there is less solar energy input per unit area. Temperatures decrease with altitude as the air becomes thinner and is less able to absorb heat. This explains why high altitude glaciers can exist near the equator.

Now test yourself

5 Explain the climatic causes of cold environments.

Answer online

Tested

Long-term global climate change

Revised

Temperatures on the surface of the Earth have varied enormously throughout history. Some of the causes of these changes include:

- **Milankovitch cycles**, in which the Earth's orbit varies every 100 000 years and the Earth's axis every 41 000 years. These are thought to be the main causes of glaciation cycles

- **solar radiation**, which varies due to the sun's energy working in cycles and can affect global temperatures

- the amount of **carbon dioxide** in the atmosphere as higher quantities lead to warmer climates. Ice core samples show that the amount of carbon dioxide in the atmosphere has fluctuated over time

Now test yourself

6 Which factors have caused global temperatures to vary over time?

Answer online

Tested

Meteorological processes

Revised

Cold climates have distinctive meteorological features:

- There are low levels of **precipitation** because of low air temperatures which cannot hold much moisture, high air pressure causing clear skies and continentality (the amount of rainfall declines away from oceans as rain-bearing depressions cannot penetrate continental interiors).

- **Wind** can vary in cold environments, but strong katabatic winds can make parts of Antarctica, for example, some of the windiest places on Earth. The wind-chill factor can make it feel colder as the wind speed increases.

- **Air temperature** can vary from 0°C to −40°C, making cold environments some of the most inhospitable places on Earth.

Now test yourself

7 Describe the distinctive meteorological features associated with cold climates.

Answer online

Tested

Answers and quick quizzes at **www.therevisionbutton.co.uk/myrevisionnotes**

Glacial and periglacial environments

Glacial and periglacial environments have changed over time:

- At the height of the last ice age (about 18 000 years ago) a large area of the northern hemisphere was covered in ice. In Britain, the ice stretched as far south as Nottingham and covered most of Ireland as well.

- Today, the extent of the ice is restricted to Antarctica, Greenland, a few areas within the Arctic circle and areas of high altitude.

> **Now test yourself**
>
> 8 How have glacial and periglacial environments changed since the last ice age?
>
> **Answer online**
>
> Tested

Distinctive landforms and landscapes

Geomorphological processes in glacial environments

Revised

The **action of ice** in a glacier can result in two main forms of erosion:

- **abrasion** — the effect that the ice has on the surface of the land beneath it. The ice carries lots of rock and sediment in it and as it moves this acts like sandpaper that grinds and scours over the surface

- **plucking** — the process whereby a glacier picks up pieces of rock as it moves down a valley slope. This happens as the base of the glacier melts and refreezes in cracks over time

Sub-aerial processes occur on the surface of the Earth and include weathering and mass movement. In a glacial environment, the key processes are:

- **frost shattering/freeze–thaw** — water seeps into cracks in the rock and then freezes, turning to ice and expanding which shatters the rock as the process continues to repeat itself over time

- **carbonation** — carbon dioxide in dissolved water forms a weak acid that then gently dissolves the rock. This process is much more effective at lower temperatures and thus has a greater impact in cold environments

- **dilation** — as the ice melts, it releases pressure on the rocks below which can cause them to fracture

> **Now test yourself**   Tested
>
> 9 Define the terms 'abrasion' and 'plucking'.
>
> 10 Explain what sub-aerial processes are and give three examples.
>
> **Answers online**

Distinctive landforms in glacial environments

Revised

Both **upland** and **lowland** glacial environments have a range of distinctive landforms, as shown in Figure 9.5.

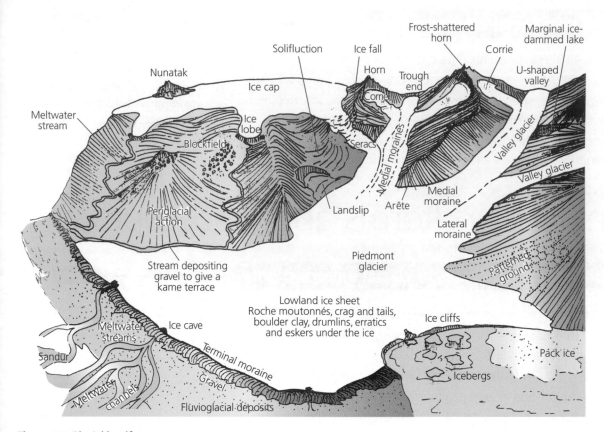

Figure 9.5 Glacial landforms

Geomorphological processes in periglacial environments   Revised ☐

Periglacial environments have permanently frozen ground to depths of over 100 m. These areas have distinctive processes:

- **frost shattering** can break apart rocks on the landscape to form a felsenmeer (a landscape littered with shattered rocks)

- **frost heave** freezes soil water just below the surface of the ground, pushing up the surface and making it bumpy and irregular

- **nivation** are the processes associated with snow, such as frost shattering and the formation of nivation hollows (where meltwater removes weathered rock). It can also contribute to the process of **slumping**

- **solifluction** is a downslope movement of rock in the summer melting period

Distinctive landforms periglacial environments

Periglacial environments have a range of distinctive landforms, as shown in Figure 9.6 and Table 9.1.

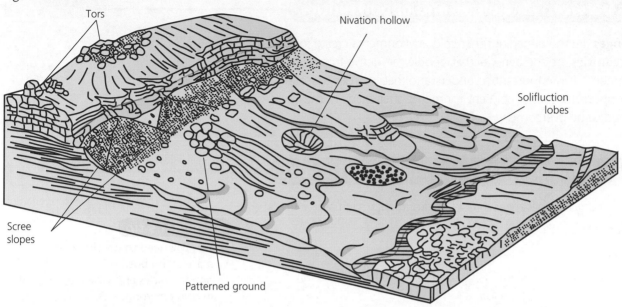

Figure 9.6 Periglacial landforms

Table 9.1 Periglacial landforms and example locations

Feature	Examples
Ice wedge casts	Giant ice wedge casts at Stanton Harcourt and Baston in Lincolnshire
Patterned ground	Stripes in Lincolnshire and Yorkshire wolds; nets and stripes on Thetford Heath, East Anglia; centre of nets correspond to chalk-loving grasses while the net reflects heathers growing on thick sands
Cryoturbation structures (deformation of sediments near surface, e.g. frost heave)	Isle of Thanet, Kent; East Anglian chalklands
Pingos	Walton Common, Cambridgeshire, where 'scars' are superimposed indicating that several cycles of ground ice growth are represented; many rampart repressions in valleys of southwest Wales, e.g. Cletwr Valley
Thermokarst scenery (slumps and depressions caused by melting ground ice)	Walton Common, Grunty Fen, Cambridgeshire
Head deposits formed through frost shattering, solifluction and sliding	Sarsen stones — streams of surface boulders running along the valley bottom of the Marlborough Downs, e.g. Coombe rock, consisting of chalk, flint and mud
Asymmetric valleys (periglacial processes acting unequally on slopes as a result of their aspect)	Chilterns
Nivation terraces (steps cut into the slope profile caused by prolonged nivation) — frost action, mass wasting and meltwater erosion beneath melting snowdrifts	Slopes of Cox Tor, Dartmoor
Tors	Pennine tors (gritstone); Stiperstones, Shropshire (quartzite); Dartmoor tors (granite)

Now test yourself

Tested

13 Describe three periglacial landforms.

Answer online

Challenges and opportunities

Links between challenges and opportunities

Challenges are the difficulties that cold environments create for people. **Opportunities** are the benefits that people can derive from cold environments. It is important to understand that in order to realise some of the opportunities that cold environments offer, many of the challenges may need to be overcome.

Past and present challenges and opportunities

There is a range of challenges in cold environments, such as:

- **relief** of the land
- **climate**
- the risk of natural hazards, such as an **avalanche** or flooding
- low agricultural productivity
- difficulty in developing and maintaining transport infrastucture

However, there is also a range of opportunities, including:

- the development of **tourism**
- **HEP** schemes
- the extraction of **mineral resources**
- oil exploration and extraction

> **Examiner's tip**
>
> You will need to develop case study material on both the challenges and opportunities and where these exist in cold environments.

> **Now test yourself**
>
> 14 Describe some of the challenges and opportunities facing cold environments.
>
> **Answer online**
>
> Tested

Overcoming the challenges

There is a range of examples that show how humans are using **technology** to overcome the challenges of cold environments, such as the following schemes in Alaska:

- oil exploration and extraction and the use of the Trans-Alaska oil pipeline to transport oil across the remote region
- the exploration of oil supplies deep in the North Slope rock using new drilling technologies
- coal mining

> **Now test yourself**
>
> 15 Give examples of how humans have used technology to overcome the challenges of cold environments.
>
> **Answer online**
>
> Tested

Using and managing cold environments

The various interest groups that are involved in the use and management of cold environments have different approaches, such as **protection/ conservation** and **sustainable management**. One example is the Alaska Conservation Foundation (ACF), which is working to ensure that Alaska is a naturally, biologically and culturally diverse wild-land that is sustainably developed. The ACF is campaigning to prevent the opening up of a strip coal mine that would destroy 17 km of salmon-spawning habitat on the edge of the Denali National Park.

> **Now test yourself**
>
> 16 Give examples of how challenges and opportunities can lead to different viewpoints in cold environments.
>
> **Answer online**
>
> Tested

Exam practice

Report-style essay

'Cold environments are increasingly coming under pressure from conflicting demands.' Discuss. [70]

Pre-released research focus

● Explore the trends in pressures and demands that cold environments experience and the players involved.

● Research a range of glacial and periglacial environments with differing demands.

Answers and quick quizzes online

Online

Examiner's summary

✔ A cold environment is an area on the Earth's surface that experiences a significant period of time when the temperature is close to or below 0°C.

✔ A cold landscape system can be understood through a systems approach.

✔ Cold landscapes have been much more extensive in the Earth's past than they are today.

✔ Britain has experienced much colder environments in the past than it does today.

✔ There are a number of climatic factors that cause cold environments.

✔ Temperatures on the surface of the Earth have varied enormously throughout history.

✔ Cold climates have distinctive meteorological features.

✔ Glacial and periglacial environments have changed over time.

✔ The action of ice in a glacier can result in two main forms of erosion: abrasian and plucking.

✔ Both upland and lowland glacial environments have a range of distinctive landforms.

✔ Periglacial areas can have permanently frozen ground, which can lead to distinctive processes.

✔ Periglacial environments have a range of distinctive landforms.

✔ There is a range of challenges and opportunities in cold environments.

✔ Various methods can be explored that highlight how humans are using technology to overcome the challenges of cold environments.

✔ There is a range of attitudes of different interest groups that are involved in the use and management of cold environments.

10 Life on the margins — the food supply problem

Global and local feast or famine

Current food supply and security issues

Revised

The World Health Organization (WHO), part of the United Nations, argues that **food security** is dependent on three things:

- **food availability** — that people have sufficient quantities of food regularly available
- **food access** — that people have sufficient resources to provide food for a nutritious diet
- **food use** — that people have adequate knowledge of basic nutrition and care, as well as adequate water and sanitation

Food security is a complex issue that links to health through the impact of malnutrition. It is dependent on economic development, the environment and trade. The key issues concerning food security are:

- **distribution** — although there is enough food produced in the world to feed everyone, there are issues associated with the distance that food travels (**food miles**)
- **production** — the needs of a rising population cannot be met by current levels of food production
- **globalisation** — and how this may impact on **food insecurity** in remote parts of the world and the impacts of global food prices
- **household food distribution** — whether all members of a household receive a fair distribution of the food available

> **Food security** is how secure the availability of food and people's access to it is in a country.
>
> **Food insecurity** is when people do not have reliable, affordable access to food.

> **Examiner's tip**
>
> Make sure you understand that food security is a complex term that has many associated issues.

> **Revision activity**
>
> Describe some of the characteristics of food supply and food security.

> **Now test yourself**
>
> 1 Explain what is meant by the term 'food security'.
>
> **Answer online**
>
> Tested

Environmental issues

Revised

Inappropriate **farming techniques** can impact on the environment. This is highlighted by problems that have resulted from increased production of common food types in the UK (e.g. milk, chicken, vegetables), such as:

- pollution from wastes, chemical use and emissions
- loss of biodiversity in the countryside
- the issue of food miles
- ethical issues such as animal welfare

> **Now test yourself**
>
> 2 Explain some of the environmental impacts of food production.
>
> **Answer online**
>
> Tested

Why food supply varies spatially

Revised

Geographical patterns of food supply vary because:

- geographical conditions (climate, flat land etc.) mean that some areas are more suited to food production (e.g. the Great Plains of the USA)

- physical factors such as lack of water, unsuitable climates or nutrient deficiencies in the soil can limit food production

Table 10.1 Factors that influence food supply variations from place to place

Human factors	Physical factors
• Accessibility of markets	• Altitude — affects temperature and water supply
• Competition, which can be healthy but is often unfair if subsidies and quotas are involved	• Aspect — slope angle
• Government action and support	• Climate — seasonal changes
• Inheritance laws, which may be gender-biased	• Hazards — tectonic, hydrometeorological and biological. For example, northern China produces 58% of the country's food crops, but in 2011 it suffered its worst drought in 50 years highlighting the increasing concern over climate change reducing agricultural production
• Land ownership systems — rented land or that without secure tenure causes insecurity	
• Market and trade patterns and regulations, which are skewed in favour of more developed economies	• Length of thermal growing season
• The role of aid agencies in both long- and short-term food supplies	• Precipitation — amount, frequency, type
• The role of businesses and TNCs, which now dominate research globally and are governed by profit margins, not necessarily food security of the poorest	• Relief — steep or waterlogged areas are less useful
	• Soil — nutrient store

Now test yourself   Tested

3 Describe three human and three physical factors that can influence food supply.

Answer online

Life on the margins   Revised

Life on the margins refers to the notion that, on a global scale, some people live in areas where access to food is not secure, such as:

- those living in areas that are traditionally perceived as regions of **famine** (e.g. Ethiopia or **Sudan**) or slums in developing world cities

- those living in areas where it is often perceived that people are food secure (e.g. New York), whereas in fact some 1.5 million people live in households with an insecure food supply

- those living in rural areas who may be food insecure due to poverty and the impact of natural hazards

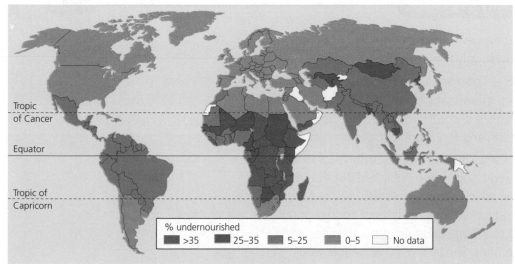

Figure 10.1 Global distribution of undernourishment, 2003–05

Now test yourself   Tested ☐

4   According to Figure 10.1, describe the global pattern of undernourishment between 2003 and 2005.

5   Explain how people living in both rural and urban areas can be food insecure.

Answers online

Revision activity

Explain some of the reasons that have caused global inequalities in food supply and security.

The complex causes of food supply inequalities

Famine and food surpluses   Revised ☐

In 2012, some 850 million people worldwide were undernourished. This has risen from a global low in 1996 of 790 million, which had followed a decade of falls in undernourishment. There is a clear distinction between areas of food surplus and those of famine. The key causes that determine this variation are summarised in Table 10.2.

Table 10.2 Factors affecting food security

Factor	Direct causes	Root causes
Economic	Income; poverty trap; land security/tenure; food supply from local producers versus national imported produce; aid; infrastructure (roads, storage, water); food hoarding	Trade restrictions; debt repayments
Social	Population growth; poor health and reduced labour (especially HIV); war (deliberate food destruction); gender equity	War and corruption; refugees and displacement; rise of middle class and changing food tastes
Environmental	Natural disasters of drought, desertification, floods, pests; overcropping and overgrazing; urban sprawl	Pollution and climate change, especially drought

Now test yourself   Tested ☐

6   Explain some of the economic, social and environmental factors affecting food security.

Answer online

The role of population pressure   Revised ☐

There are two main contrasting viewpoints on population pressure and the expected impact on food supply (Figure 10.2):

● the **Malthusian model** — Thomas Malthus wrote a paper in 1798 arguing that as population grew it would outstrip food supply; natural checks such as disease, famine and war would reduce the population in order to bring population and food supply back into balance

● the **Boserup Model** — Esther Boserup was a Danish economist who worked for the United Nations. She published *The Conditions of Natural Growth* in 1965 in which she opposed the view of Malthus. She argued that food production does not limit or control population growth. Instead, she said that population growth influences and improves agricultural methods. She believed that people would not let themselves succumb to disease or famine, but would invent technological solutions to the problem

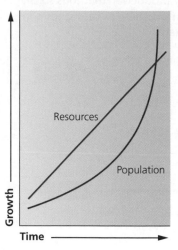

(a) Malthusian model
Population growth outstrips resources

(b) Boserup model
Resources, inventions and technology keep pace with population demands

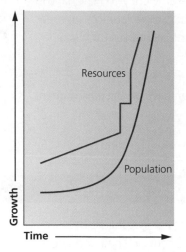

Figure 10.2 Two models of the relationship between food supplies and demand

Now test yourself

7 Draw labelled diagrams explaining the Malthusian and Boserup models.

Answer online

Tested ☐

Impacts of attempts to increase global food supply   Revised ☐

Farming techniques have a range of impacts on the natural environment. Some are more damaging than others, as shown in Table 10.3.

Table 10.3 Farming inputs and outputs

Input	Purpose	Outputs — environmental impacts
Machinery, e.g. tractors and combine harvesters, and air transport for perishables	To replace human or animal labour and increase efficiency	Pollution — increased fossil fuel use for transport and refrigeration
		Increased food miles and packaging
		Soil compaction and erosion
		Loss of biodiversity in wetlands, hedgerows and forests
		Trawling impacts on marine ecosystems and non-target species, e.g. dolphin and albatross
Chemical fertilisers, especially nitrogen products	To increase yield by providing high levels of plant nutrients	Pollution — eutrophication of water by agricultural runoff
		Loss of biodiversity, e.g. sugar cane in the Caribbean
Pesticides	To remove insects and other pests, which could reduce yields	Toxic chemicals such as DDT enter the food chain and cause damage to organisms, which were not the intended 'victim' of the chemical
Herbicides and fungicides	To remove weeds, which take up space and use up nutrients, and reduce fungal diseases that reduce yields	
Antibiotics	To increase resistance to disease in livestock and fish and increase yields	Antibiotic-resistant bacteria and the danger of epidemic outbreaks
		Fears for human health due to consuming meat
Animal or fish feed	To increase the density of animals/fish kept in a given area	Increased demand for food crops to be used to feed livestock and therefore increased pressure to clear areas (e.g. forests) to produce more crops, especially soya
		Waste products from animal slurry are highly toxic
		Methane from livestock is a potent global-warming gas
		Intensively reared cattle are fed diets rich in protein and energy — for every hectare of feedlot in the UK, two more are farmed overseas to meet its needs

Cuba has become 90% self-sufficient in the production of fresh fruit and vegetables. Following the collapse of the Soviet Union, oil supplies to Cuba were restricted and many people turned to self-sufficiency. In Havana, the capital city, almost 200 urban allotments known as *organiponicos* were set up, which produce more than 4 million tonnes of vegetables each year.

Now test yourself   Tested

8   Describe a range of impacts that farming can have on the environment.

Answer online

Who has been most affected by food insecurity?   Revised

You will need to develop a range of case studies that investigate the nature of groups of people vulnerable to food insecurity. The Food and Agriculture Organization (FAO) suggests that food security is vulnerable when any of the following criteria apply:

● if places have suffered prolonged human crises such as war and/or natural disasters
● if weak governance or public administration have impacted on food supplies
● if there are unsustainable livelihood systems and poor food security outcomes
● if there has been a breakdown of local institutions

Table 10.4 identifies countries that would make suitable case studies for detailed research.

Table 10.4 Suitable case study countries

Data for 1996–2010	Years of natural disasters	Years of human disasters	Years of combined natural and human disasters	Emergency aid as a % of all aid
Afghanistan	–	5	10	20
DRC	–	15	–	27
Ethiopia	2	2	11	21
Haiti	11	1	3	11
Sudan	–	5	10	62

Source: www.fao.org

Now test yourself

9   Which factors does the FAO state can affect food security?

Answer online
Tested

Desertification and life at the margin of survival

Desertification and its scale and impact   Revised

Desertification is mainly caused by:
● **land clearance,** when vegetation is chopped down in large numbers, having an adverse effect on the local ecosystem which cannot later recover

Desertification is the process whereby once-fertile land gradually becomes degraded and begins to form a desert.

- **drought**, which is a long-term lack of rainfall that leads to plants dying
- improper or **inappropriate farming techniques** and overuse of the land for farming or grazing, which can exhaust the soil so it cannot later recover

The causes of desertification can be both human and physical, as shown in Figure 10.3.

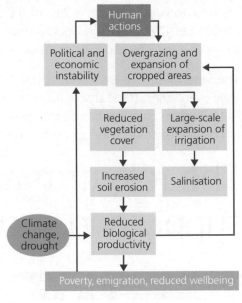

Figure 10.3 Simplified causes of desertification

Revision activity

How is desertification threatening life at the margins?

Now test yourself   Tested ☐

10 Explain what is meant by the term 'desertification'.
11 What are the major causes of desertification?

Answers online

Dryland ecosystems   Revised ☐

Drylands are home to over 2 billion people and cover about 41% of the Earth's land surface. They are places where the production of crops is limited by the amount of available water. Dryland areas are particularly susceptible to desertification because of their inherent lack of water, which can put the ecosystem under a huge amount of stress. People living in these areas often practise nomadic farming, but sophisticated irrigation systems allow much more intensive farming in some dryland areas such as in Israel, which uses water from the Sea of Galilee through the Israeli National Water Carrier pipeline to irrigate large areas of land for farming.

> **Drylands** are arid areas with low levels of rainfall.

Now test yourself

12 What are dryland areas?

Answer online

Tested ☐

The vulnerability of drylands   Revised ☐

There are a number of human factors that have made drylands vulnerable:

- people have overused the natural vegetation cover through improper management
- there has been poorly planned conversion of pasture to arable land through irrigation schemes
- soil quality has become degraded through salinisation and the input of chemicals

The impacts of this land degradation can lead to the migration of people away from areas under stress, as well as the risk of famine and political unrest.

Now test yourself

13 How can people impact on dryland areas?

Answer online

Tested ☐

Food production and supply   Revised ☐

Food production usually requires enormous amounts of water:

- it takes about 1500 litres of water to produce 1 kg of wheat
- It takes 10 times this — 15 000 litres of water — to produce 1 kg of beef

Irrigated agriculture uses only 20% of the total agricultural land and contributes 40% to the total food produced worldwide. However, this is at a cost of using 70% of our available water supplies each year.

The Sahel in Africa is a region that is suffering from desertification. Large-scale overgrazing in the area and a heavy dependency on the limited water supplies have led to extensive desertification. Rainfall in the region has continued to decrease, exacerbating the problem.

Now test yourself

14 Explain some of the impacts of desertification on food supplies.

Answer online

Tested

The role of management in food supply and security

Management techniques and strategies
Revised

Food management techniques are the policies and technology that are put in place to ensure that there is an adequate food supply. **Food management strategies** are the overall aims of trying to ensure that there is an adequate food supply. They are not aimed at just increasing food production; they also focus on other strategies such as **fair trade** and **food distribution**.

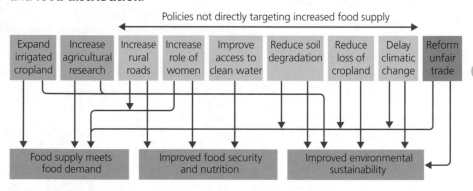

Figure 10.4 The spectrum of strategies to tackle food insecurity

Now test yourself

15 What are food management strategies and how do food management techniques differ?

Answer online

Tested

International efforts
Revised

There is a range of strategies for providing global food supplies:

- **technological solutions** such as the Green Revolution or the Gene Revolution
- **low cost (intermediate technology) solutions** such as the use of diguettes in Burkina Faso in the Sahel or the small dams project in Ethiopia
- **environmental solutions** such as organic farming in Cuba

Examiner's tip

You need to have a case study to support each of these strategies for improving global food supplies.

Now test yourself

16 Describe the three main food strategies that exist.

Answer online

Tested

Effective initiatives
Revised

A range of organisations is involved in food supply in marginal areas, as shown in Table 10.5.

Table 10.5 Players in the delivery of strategies

Player	Role in sustaining life of the margins	Examples
Individuals, e.g. farmers	Direct producers of food Communities harbour stores of valuable local knowledge, coping strategies and innovation Their cooperation is critical to ensure environmental sustainability	Role of fair trade organisations and impact on individuals Local organic farms, LEAF
Governments	Provide funding for agricultural research and development Important in creating political and economic conditions to ensure stability of food supply Response during times of crisis	Large-scale rehabilitation projects, e.g. China's Great Green Wall, Japan or UK overseas aid projects Legal and conservation frameworks
Businesses and TNCs	Research and investment into new farming methods and technologies Resource exploitation and trade in cash crops, fertilisers and farm machinery Profit motives	The development of GM crop varieties such as Golden Rice Monsanto (TNC) Toyota Motor Corporation
NGOs and foundations	Community-level support for farmers in the developing world Education, training and skills providers Many promote social equity such as female empowerment	Implementation of sustainable dryland farming in the Sudan by Practical Action Emergency aid, e.g. Oxfam International Alliance Against Hunger
Research organisations	Conduct scientific research on new crop varieties and farm systems Not-for-profit motives Education and skills training of farmers	The development of HYVs by the International Rice Research Institute AGRA's work on a Green Revolution in Africa
IGOs such as UNEP and FAO	Promote international cooperation Implement global actions such as the Millennium Development Goals Monitoring and research to identify problems and seek solutions Development assistance and aid to the developing world	World Bank's Global Food Crisis Response Program 1994 UN Convention to Combat Desertification
Watchdog pressure groups	Research and information-gathering Lobbying agencies	World Resources Institute Community Food Security Coalition (USA) Sustain

Now test yourself

Tested ☐

17 Describe some of the organisations involved in marginal food supply areas.

Answer online

Sustainable strategies

Revised ☐

There are three main aims that **sustainable food management** should meet. It should:

- meet the increase in food demand
- provide food security for all
- be environmentally sustainable

A variety of management strategies are designed to be sustainable, such as:

- **fair trade** — companies pay sustainable prices (which must never fall lower than market price) to farmers

- **organic farming** — farmers use traditional farming techniques such as crop rotation alongside non-chemical fertilisers and biological pest control
- **aquaculture** — farming fish in ponds and lagoons

Tested ☐

18 What are the main aims of sustainable food management?

Answer online

Revision activity

Explain how effective some management strategies are in sustaining life at the margins.

Exam practice

Report-style essay

To what extent do food security issues vary across the world? [70]

Pre-released research focus

- Explore why food security varies spatially.
- Research a range of rural and urban locations experiencing food security issues.

Answers and quick quizzes online

Online ☐

Examiner's summary

- ✔ Food security is a complex term to define.
- ✔ Inappropriate farming techniques can impact on the environment.
- ✔ Geographical patterns of food supply vary worldwide.
- ✔ Some people live in areas where access to food is not secure.
- ✔ There is a clear distinction between areas of food surplus and those of famine.
- ✔ There are two main contrasting viewpoints on population pressure and the expected impact on food supply: the Malthusian model and the Boserup model.
- ✔ Farming techniques have a range of impacts on the natural environment.
- ✔ There is a range of places that are vulnerable to food insecurity.
- ✔ Desertification is the process whereby once-fertile land gradually becomes degraded and begins to form a desert.

- ✔ Drylands are arid areas that have low levels of rainfall.
- ✔ There are a number of human factors that have made dryland areas vulnerable.
- ✔ Food production usually requires enormous amounts of water.
- ✔ Food management strategies are the overall aims to try to ensure that there is an adequate food supply.
- ✔ There is a range of strategies for providing global food supplies, including technological, low cost and environmental solutions.
- ✔ There is a range of organisations involved in marginal food supply areas.
- ✔ A range of management strategies are designed to be sustainable, including fair trade, organic farming and aquaculture.

11 The world of cultural diversity

Defining culture and identifying its value

Definitions of culture

Revised

Culture is a dynamic term that can evolve and change. It represents a system of shared values in a society that influence lifestyles and sets boundaries for behaviour and interaction with others. The term is complex and can be used in a number of ways, such as when referring to arts and media: high culture, for example, can be used in the context of art, opera or classical music, whereas popular culture refers to more current cultural affairs such as pop music, television soap operas and sport.

Ethnicity means belonging to a group of people who share a common national or cultural tradition. **Cultural beliefs** are the commonly held values within a cultural group. **Cultural landscapes** are defined by the World Heritage Committee as distinct geographical areas that have been 'designed and created intentionally by man' or a place in which a natural feature has a religious, artistic or cultural significance.

> **Culture** is defined as the behaviours and beliefs of a social, ethnic or age group.

> **Examiner's tip**
>
> A number of complex definitions need to be learnt for this option. It is important that you can recall them quickly and use them correctly in the exam.

> **Now test yourself**
>
> 1 Explain why 'culture' is such a difficult term to define.
>
> **Answer online**
>
> Tested

Human cultures and cultural landscapes

Revised

A number of different facets make up culture, as shown in Figure 11.1. Culture can also have an impact on the geography of a place and people can attach cultural value to places that they identify with:

- **Traditional cultural landscapes** are places that reflect community beliefs or artistic and traditional customs, such as Westminster in London.

- **Technoscapes** are places that are centres of high-tech industry with associated high-tech architecture, such as Cupertino in California (the home of Apple, Oracle and Hewlett Packard) or the Cambridge Science Park.

- **Ethnoscapes** are places that exhibit ethnic representations from a group of people who have migrated from another part of the world, such as Southall in west London or Chinatown in San Francisco.

> **Revision activity**
>
> Explain the nature and value of culture in terms of people and places.

> **Now test yourself**
>
> 2 Explain what is meant by the terms 'technoscape' and 'ethnoscape'.
>
> 3 Draw a diagram showing the core components of culture.
>
> **Answers online**
>
> Tested

Figure 11.1 The core components of culture

Vulnerable cultures and landscapes

Revised

The cultures of some groups of people can come under threat through direct action such as:

- genocide, in which a particular group of people is deliberately targeted for destruction for political, religious or ideological reasons, such as the Rwandan genocide of 1994
- ethnocide, which is the focused destruction of the culture of a people rather than the people themselves, such as China has done in **Tibet**

Culture and cultural landscapes can also be vulnerable to more indirect degradation:

- **Tourism** has exposed remote **Bhutan** to external cultures as people from elsewhere visit. This means that local cultures can become threatened due to the drive for economic development and the aspiration to adopt Western culture and values.
- Changes in the way that people earn a living can also lead to changes in the cultural landscape, such as the demise of rural cultures as society has become less dependent on primary production for employment.

> **Now test yourself**
>
> 4 Describe some ways in which culture can be threatened.
>
> **Answer online**
>
> Tested

The value of cultural diversity

Revised

Cultural diversity refers to the variety of different cultures that exists in parts of the world. Many places value their cultural diversity and this is often the case in large metropolitan cities such as London and New York where people from many different nationalities and backgrounds converge.

The value of some cultural landscapes and sites is protected by the World Heritage Centre, part of the United Nations Educational, Scientific and Cultural Organization (UNESCO), which has created the World Heritage List of 745 culturally significant places that have been protected. These include Uluru-Kata Tjuta National Park in Australia and the Loire Valley in France.

> **Now test yourself**
>
> 5 How is cultural diversity valued?
>
> **Answer online**
>
> Tested

The geography of culture

Cultural homogeneity

Revised

Some countries are culturally more **homogenous** than others and this can often be explained through geographical and socio-economic factors:

- **Japan** can be regarded as culturally homogenous because 99% of the population is Japanese and more than 87% of people follow the Shinto religion.
- **Iceland** is another country considered to be culturally homogenous, with 99% of people living in urban areas and 60% living within the greater Reykjavik area.

This is in contrast to countries like the **UK** where the colonial past has meant that many people from former British colonies have chosen to migrate to the UK, building up a culturally diverse population including people from almost every continent.

> **Homogenous** means being similar or uniform. In cultural terms, it refers to societies with little ethnic or cultural attitude diversity.

> **Now test yourself**
>
> 6 Describe how some countries can be considered to be culturally homogenous.
>
> **Answer online**
>
> Tested

The urban/rural cultural divide

Revised

Cultural diversity tends to be more pronounced in major urban areas of the world such as London or New York. This is because:

- cities can be key 'switched-on' places where there is clear evidence of economic success, which attracts migrants
- cities are often key transport hubs, with ports or airports where new arrivals often settle
- migrants may cluster in cities where they feel welcome among others from the same ethnic background
- cities allow new migrants to blend in and differences are often more accepted
- there is a wider range of economic opportunities

Rural areas, however, tend to be less culturally diverse because there are fewer employment opportunities and they are often more remote and isolated.

> **Revision activity**
>
> Give reasons why culture can vary spatially.

> **Now test yourself**
>
> 7 Why are urban areas more culturally diverse than rural areas?
>
> **Answer online**
>
> Tested

Attitudes to cultural diversity

Revised

Governments and other key players can impact on cultural diversity:

- Impacts can be negative, such as in **Tibet** where the Chinese government has introduced a policy that all primary school lessons and textbooks should be in Chinese by 2015 in order to help Tibetans integrate into Chinese society. This has led to protests by citizens who believe that Tibetan is being downgraded as a language.
- Impacts can also be positive, such as those relating to the Society for the Protection of Nature in **Israel** which has been set up to preserve Israel's natural resources, environment, natural assets and unique landscape and has a particular focus on preserving the ancient biblical landscape of the country.

> **Now test yourself**
>
> 8 Using examples, explain how governments and key players can impact on cultural diversity.
>
> **Answer online**
>
> Tested

Cultural imperialism

Revised

Cultural imperialism is the notion that a more dominant culture becomes imposed on another culture. **McDonaldisation** is the term given to the consumerist culture dominant in the USA and Western Europe, which has spread globally. It can be illustrated through the physical appearance of McDonald's stores and other Western brands around the world in places such as China, Morocco and Peru, as well as through the spread of Western attitudes as people become focused on:

- resource consumption and consumerism
- a political focus on Western-style democracy
- a belief in the benefits of technology
- the influence of American media and popular culture
- a reliance on a globalised economy

> **Now test yourself**
>
> 9 What is meant by the term 'cultural imperialism'?
>
> 10 Explain some of the impacts of McDonaldisation.
>
> **Answers online**
>
> Tested

The impact of globalisation on cultural diversity

The significance of globalisation

Revised

There is a range of opinions about the impact that globalisation may have on cultural diversity, which are summarised in Figure 11.2.

		Globalisation is not new or global: it maintains switched-on areas of Europe, North America and Japan and excludes switched-off places — most of sub-Saharan Africa. The rich get richer
Reduction of cultural diversity with globalisation	Process of globalisation forces countries and governments to adapt and change in uncomfortable ways	

← Pessimistic **hyperglobalisers** **Transformationalists** **Sceptics** →

Increasing power of TNCs. The rise of a global consumer culture and loss of local and national identity	Formation of the EU super bloc to maintain Europe's power. USA and UK reaction to the 2008 global financial crisis by nationalisation, bailouts, subsidies — a reversal of decades of a market-led economy	85% of world trade is still between developed countries. Increasing divide between rich and poor

Figure 11.2 The globalisation debate

Now test yourself

11 Summarise the range of opinions that the impact of globalisation may have on cultural diversity.

Answer online

Tested

Global media corporations

Revised

Global media corporations such as **Disney** and **Viacom** can have disproportionate power because of their ability to convey their cultural values and attitudes. These media corporations have worldwide audiences and can spread cultural attitudes and beliefs. Many of these organisations have disputed this idea, claiming that no one is forced to buy, watch, listen to or use their products.

Examiner's tip

Research a global media organisation such as News International so that you can use this as a case study in your exam.

Now test yourself

Tested

12 Describe the positive and negative impacts that global media corporations may have on culture.

Answer online

Cultural globalisation and hybrid culture

Revised

Cultural globalisation often takes place in **local contexts** and this can give rise to distinctive 'glocalised' forms of fashion, music and film in which global culture has fused with local culture:

- The **Bollywood** phenomenon has arisen from the fusion of Indian films made in Mumbai with a more American (Hollywood) style of presentation in which the Hindi language is mixed with English.

- The internet has given rise to a new language with the introduction of blogs, Facebook, Twitter and a whole host of **social media** that have contributed towards the development of an internet culture.

Now test yourself

13 Using examples, explain how cultural globalisation has given rise to 'glocalised' cultural forms.

Answer online

Tested

The impacts of a globalised consumerist society

Increasing wealth and globalisation can have both positive and negative influences on people, culture and landscapes:

- poorer people around the world look outward and focus on becoming part of a mainstream globalised society
- local cultural traditions weaken as people see themselves as part of the global society
- many parts of the world can become similar in appearance as global retailers and corporations expand
- people may find that consumerism, and the drive to own more, impacts on their life satisfaction as they strive to own the next 'must-have' item.

Revision activity

What impact is globalisation having on culture?

Now test yourself

14 Summarise the impacts of a globalised consumerist culture.

Answer online

Tested

Cultural attitudes to the environment

Different cultural attitudes

Revised

The environment is defined as the surroundings in which people live and is often regarded as the natural world and its functions. There are four main cultural attitudes to the environment:

- **techno-centric view** — the environment is a resource for humans to use and a sink for waste products
- **accommodation view** — the impacts of exploitation can be reduced through finance, technology and smart techniques
- **social ecology view** — a new system is needed with a focus on community and local ideas such as organic farming
- **deep ecology view** — a return to pre-industrial attitudes towards the environment in which nature dominates

Now test yourself

15 Summarise the four main cultural views on the environment.

Answer online

Tested

How different cultures value the landscape

Revised

Different cultures also have different attitudes that affect the way in which the landscape is valued in terms of **exploitation** and **protection**. The landscape may be:

- valued as sacred and thus preserved
- an opportunity for leisure and recreation, thus being conserved but risking degradation through pollution
- considered 'alive' and a source of life and therefore protected
- a source of profit leading to degradation and possible destruction

Different cultures also have different attitudes towards the notion of **sustainability**. Some cultures, such as the UK government, regard it as an approach toward social equity and public participation, whereas others regard it as a 'green' concept focusing on environmental issues.

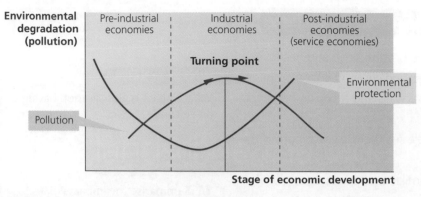

Figure 11.3 Attitudes to environmental protection

Anthropocentric cultural values

Revised

Human cultural values in the Western world have developed an **anthropocentric attitude** in which humans tend to see themselves as dominant over physical and ecological aspects of the broader cultural landscape.

There has been a continued trend in Western culture towards a growing culture of **consumption**. It is often commented on in the media that the growth of emerging markets such as India and China will see these countries adopt a more consumerist culture as more people have access to wealth. Western culture has led to a belief that greater wealth leads to more material possessions, which in turn make people happier. There is an expected view that the development of once-poor nations will see a rise in consumerism as people strive to become happier through materialism.

This has also led to the development of **counter-cultures** that spurn such views. These include ecological movements that believe in a more harmonious relationship with our natural environment, as well as anti-capitalist movements.

Environmentalism and consumer capitalism

Revised

Most people in the world live with capitalism and consumerism. However, capitalism brings forth an economic and political system that can lead to the destruction of the environment because of the:

- accountability of businesses to shareholders rather than to people or the environment
- continual drive for profits, regardless of the impact on the environment
- marginalisation of poor people who tend to have a greater reliance on the natural environment

However, despite the growing nature of consumerism, many people and cultures are now beginning to display concerns about **biodiversity loss**, **global warming** and the impacts of **environmental change**.

Online

Exam practice

Report-style essay

'Cultural attitudes determine how landscapes and environments are valued.' Discuss. [70]

Pre-released research focus

● Explore the attitudes of different cultures to the environment and landscape.

● Research a range of landscapes and environments to see how these attitudes may affect their value as shown by management and use.

Answers and quick quizzes online

Examiner's summary

✔ Culture is a complex term to define.

✔ There is a range of human cultures and cultural landscapes.

✔ Cultures and landscapes can be threatened in a variety of ways.

✔ Cultural diversity refers to the variety of different cultures that can exist in parts of the world.

✔ Some countries are culturally more homogenous than others.

✔ Cultural diversity tends to be more pronounced in major urban areas of the world.

✔ Governments and other key players can impact on cultural diversity.

✔ Cultural imperialism is impacting on local cultures.

✔ There is a wide range of opinions about the impacts of globalisation on culture.

✔ Global media corporations can convey dominant cultural values and attitudes.

✔ Increasing wealth and globalisation can have both positive and negative influences on people, culture and landscapes.

✔ There are four main cultural views on the environment.

✔ Different cultures also have different attitudes to the environment.

✔ An anthropocentric attitude towards the world has developed in which humans regard themselves as dominant over the natural environment.

✔ Capitalism has led to an economic and political system that has negative impacts for the environment.

12 Pollution and human health at risk

Defining the risks to human health

In this option, you need to understand that health is a concern for people at a range of scales from personal to global, that health can have a key impact on quality of life and that it also can affect economic development. Health risk can be related to economic development (either through transmissible disease or environmental pollution) and the spread of this risk follows geographical patterns and features.

Mortality is concerned with death — it is the condition of being mortal or susceptible to death. **Morbidity** is concerned with illness, disease, disability and poor health. It is the condition of poor health from any cause.

There is a range of health risks from short term to chronic. Short-term health risks can broadly be seen to have a greater impact in low-income countries. They may often be associated with infectious diseases, including:

- vectored diseases such as malaria (transmitted by mosquitoes)
- non-vectored diseases such as influenza (transmitted from person to person)

Infectious diseases can often cause acute health risks with a rapid onset or intense symptoms. These can be split into:

- **endemic diseases**, which have persisted in a geographical area for a long period of time
- **epidemic diseases**, which have a widespread distribution
- **pandemic diseases**, which are prevalent throughout the whole world

Chronic health risks tend to be more common in middle- and high-income countries. They are often caused by the lifestyle that people lead or by our genes. There are a host of non-communicable diseases such as cancer, diabetes and cardiovascular disease that fall into this category. The WHO estimates that these types of diseases account for about 60% of all global deaths.

> **Typical mistake**
>
> It is easy to confuse mortality and morbidity. Make sure you are clear on the use of key terms in your report, particularly for the D component.

> **Revision activity**
>
> Describe a range of risks to human health.

> **Now test yourself** — Tested
>
> 1 Explain the difference between mortality and morbidity.
> 2 List short-term health risks to people and indicate whether they are vectored or non-vectored.
> 3 Explain the difference between an epidemic and a pandemic.
>
> Answers online

Patterns of health risk

On a global scale there is a range of health risks that can affect people at a range of scales, from regional, national and global:

- **At a regional scale** — levels of healthcare vary considerably within countries. In the USA a free market, fee-paying approach to healthcare exists. This creates poor access for low-income people. The Kansas City Free Health Clinic is one of the largest free health clinics in the USA and it provides quality healthcare services for residents of Kansas City at no charge.

- **At a national scale** — in the UK questions are frequently raised about the differences in the quality of healthcare provided by the NHS in different parts of the country (the 'postcode lottery'). The Department of Health published an atlas of health variations across the UK in 2010, which showed that there were clear variations between the 152 primary care trusts in both health spending and health outcomes.

- **At a global scale** — health risks can vary depending on national wealth (Table 12.1).

Table 12.1 Health risks according to national wealth

World Bank grouping	Average gross national income (GNI) per person per year	Health characteristics
Low-income countries	US$935 or less	Countries with high mortality and morbidity rates 25% of the population reach 70 years of age 33% of deaths are of those under 14 years of age Infectious diseases (especially HIV/AIDS, tuberculosis and malaria) are the most common cause of death Cardiovascular disease is the single main cause of death Examples include Kenya and Bangladesh
Middle-income countries	US$936–US$11455	50% of the population reach 70 years of age Chronic diseases combined with HIV/AIDS are the most common cause of death Examples include China and Brazil
High-income countries	US$11456 or more	Countries with low mortality and usually with low morbidity rates At least 66% of the population reach 70 years of age Chronic diseases (including cancers, diabetes and dementia) are the most common cause of death Examples include the UK and the USA

4 List some of the ways that health risks vary on a global scale.

Answer online

Health risk patterns over time

The epidemiological transition model in Table 12.2 shows how health risks vary with increasing economic development in a country.

Table 12.2 Epidemiological transition model

Measure	Stage 1: The age of pestilence and famine	Stage 2: The age of receding pandemics	Stage 3: The age of chronic diseases	Stage 4: The age of emerging/ re-emerging infectious diseases
Mortality	High and fluctuating	Declining progressively	Continues to decline and begins to stabilise at a low level	Remains low but may begin to increase slightly
Morbidity	High rates of infectious, acute diseases	Epidemic peaks become less frequent or disappear	The disappearance of infectious is diseases is replaced by degenerative and human-induced diseases	The emergence of delayed degenerative diseases, new infectious diseases and the re-emergence of 'old' diseases
Life expectancy	Under 30 years	Rises considerably, from under 30 to over 50	Rises gradually until it exceeds 50 years	Continues to rise above 70 years
Examples of health risk	Measles, smallpox, malaria, typhoid, cholera, tuberculosis, diarrhoea and pneumonia	Cancer, heart disease and respiratory diseases		Alzheimer's, HIV/AIDS, SARS, tuberculosis and measles

Now test yourself

Tested

5 Explain how health risk patterns change over time.

Answer online

Examiner's tip

A model such as the epidemiological model in Table 12.2 can be a good template for inclusion in the report-style essay, particularly when the exam question focuses on changes in health risk over time.

Quality of life and economic development

The WHO states that 'good health is essential to human welfare and to sustained economic and social development'. Health risk can impact on:

- an individual's quality of life through poor health, a shorter life expectancy, the ability to earn a living and negative effects for family members
- a country's economic development through the loss of time at work and productivity

The complex causes of health risk

The causes of health risk

The causes of health risk can be divided into:

- internal causes, such as your genes, lifestyle choices or employment risks
- external causes, such as the environmental conditions to which you are exposed (e.g. pollution) or the role of government strategies to prevent health risks (e.g. banning smoking in public buildings)

Now test yourself

6 Explain the difference between internal and external causes of health risk.

Answer online

Tested

Socio-economic status and health

Revised

Spatial variations in health can often be influenced by socio-economic status as wealth can directly influence:

- diet and nutrition
- sanitation and access to clean water
- medical treatment opportunities
- employment types and work-place dangers
- education level

It is also possible that someone's standard of living may influence whether they are more or less susceptible to some health risks, such as:

- overuse of antibiotics
- inadequate public health services
- migration and exposure to health risks

Revision activity

Explain how the causes of health risk can be determined by socio-economic factors.

Now test yourself

7 How can wealth influence health risk?

Answer online

Tested

Geographical features

Revised

There are several ways in which geographical factors are important in influencing the spread of disease. Diseases are often linked to locational factors or influenced by environmental conditions in a particular location.

John Snow's study of cholera in the 1850s involved plotting the distribution of cholera deaths according to where people lived in an area clustered around a particular water pump in Soho, London. Snow made a positive link from his study between infected water pumps and cholera cases. Stagnant water in tropical areas raises malaria risk as it provides a breeding ground for mosquitoes. In some cases, infectious diseases can be carried along transport and trade routes. Healthcare is not equally available to everyone: there is an inequality of healthcare services in relation to population (number of doctors per person, location of hospitals) and inequalities of access to these facilities (travel times, transport availability and cost).

Examiner's tip

Research the impacts of other environmental factors that can influence the spread of disease, such as climate, and human factors, such as air travel.

Now test yourself

8 How can environmental conditions affect health risk?

9 Describe the influence of human factors that affect health risk.

Answers online

Tested

Health risk causes and patterns

Revised

You need to understand that many diseases may follow a diffusion model, as shown in Figure 12.1.

 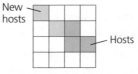 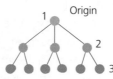

(a) Expansion diffusion: the disease spreads from one place but remains concentrated there

(b) Relocation diffusion, e.g. some types of flu: the disease moves from place to place

(c) Contagious diffusion, e.g. measles: direct contact is needed to pass on the disease

(d) Hierarchical diffusion, e.g. HIV, SARS: the disease spreads from one large centre to a number of smaller centres

Figure 12.1 Types of spatial diffusion

Pollution and health risk

Pollution types

Revised ☐

Environmental health risks can be divided into:

- one-off (**incidental**) pollution incidents, which are moved by water or air, such as the Deepwater Horizon oil spill in the USA in 2010 or the Bhopal gas leak in India in 1984

- longer-term (**sustained**) pollution, such as the long-term risk of passive smoking which has led to the banning of smoking in public places in the UK or the risk of developing skin cancer from ozone depletion

Incidental and sustained pollution

Revised ☐

The health risks from incidental and sustained pollution are many and varied:

- The Deepwater Horizon oil spill led to a number of immediate casualties, with health risks from heat stress and chemical exposures, but these were limited to the immediate geographical area. A detailed report is available at **www.cdc.gov/niosh/hhe/reports/pdfs/2010-0115-0129-3138.pdf**.

- The Bhopal disaster led to more than 8000 immediate deaths followed by many more as the gas cloud spread from the initial blast point.

- The long-term effects of the ozone hole discovered over Antarctica are still not fully known. Australia suffers from the highest skin cancer rates in the world, which led to the Slip! Slop! Slap! campaign to reduce the number of cases.

Pollution, economic development and changing health risks

Revised ☐

Kuznets' environmental curve (Figure 12.2) suggests that there is a relationship between environmental quality and economic development. Simon Kuznets (1901–85) was a Russian-born American economist who argued that as a country develops there will be an increase in pollution and associated health risks, but after a certain average income is attained those risks will decrease.

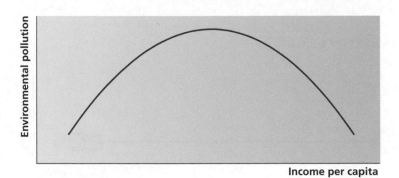

Figure 12.2 Kuznets' environmental curve

Pollution fatigue

Revised

Pollution fatigue is when people become so 'tired' of the risks from pollution that it leads to public pressure for industry or governments to take effective action either to manage the incident better or to avoid future incidents:

- In the case of the Deepwater Horizon oil spill, many people living on the Florida coast were unwilling to let the pollution impact on them, so they forced BP to take immediate action to try to contain the spill and provide a long-term clean-up operation.

- In the case of passive smoking, there was a build-up of momentum in the UK that led to the banning of smoking in public places and cigarettes being on display in shops, and a campaign for unbranded packaging.

Now test yourself

15 What is pollution fatigue?

Answer online

Tested

Managing the health risk

Socio-economic and environmental impacts

Revised

The impacts of health risk can be both short term and long term on both individuals and groups of people. Some examples of these impacts are given in Table 12.3.

Table 12.3 Short-term and long-term impacts of health risk

Short-term impacts	Long-term impacts
Working days lost when people are ill	Impact on the economy as large numbers of people fall victim to one type of disease, e.g. HIV/AIDS
	Can lead to lower tax revenue for governments, resulting in lower spending on healthcare and disease prevention
Lost school days as children are ill or looking after sick parents	Can impact on the economy as there are fewer skilled workers available
	Women are disproportionately affected as they often take on the carer role and therefore the lack of education for women can continue the cycle of poor health
Cost of treating sick members of the family or buying preventative measures such as mosquito nets	Cost to government of providing healthcare facilities. For example, malaria can absorb 40% of healthcare costs in some countries
Death of family member and associated costs	In the case of HIV/AIDS, this can lead to the loss of working-age adults who would normally be the cornerstone of the economy

16 Explain some of the short-term and long-term impacts of a disease such as HIV/AIDS.

Answer online

Management strategies and policies · Revised ☐

Some health risks are harder to manage than others (Table 12.4).

Table 12.4 Ease of management of health risks

Easier	Harder
Infectious diseases linked to problems of the built environment (e.g. water supply, sewage, housing, food supply) such as cholera	Chronic diseases such as heart disease, obesity and depression
Short-term health shocks such as mental and physical traumas linked to disasters	Incurable infectious diseases such as HIV/AIDS

17 Why do you think some health risks are easier to manage than others?

Answer online

Tested ☐

Agencies involved · Revised ☐

The WHO is the most important single global advisory health organisation. It has the authority within the United Nations for directing and coordinating global health issues. It provides leadership on global health matters, shapes health research and monitors and assesses global health trends.

18 What is the role of the WHO?

Answer online

> **Examiner's tip**
>
> Make sure you know the role of the WHO in formulating health policies around the world and how it works with other organisations (TNCs and NGOs) to manage health risk.

Managing health risk effectively · Revised ☐

Uganda is a model for Africa in the fight against HIV/AIDS. Government leadership, coupled with broad-based partnerships and effective public education campaigns, all contributed to a dramatic decline in the number of people living with HIV/AIDS in the 1990s.

Following the G8 summit in 2005, the world's wealthiest countries created the Highly Indebted Poor Countries (HIPC) initiative, which cancelled debts from many of the world's poorest countries. Since its debt cancellations, health management in Uganda has had a significant financial boost and the Ugandan government is committed to a national healthcare system including the abolition of fees for basic healthcare services:

- the proportion of government spending on health has risen from 7.3% to 8.9%
- per capita expenditure has increased by 70% from US$45 in 2000 to US$71 in 2006

However, there is still much progress to be made: Uganda's healthcare is still ranked as one of the worst in the world by the WHO, coming 186th out of 191 countries.

> **Revision activity**
>
> Describe some of the ways in which health risks can be managed.

Now test yourself

Tested ☐

19 How successful has Uganda been in managing health risk?

Answer online

Exam practice

Report-style essay

To what extent do health risk causes and patterns vary? [70]

Pre-released research focus

● Explore the complex causes of health risk and any links to socio-economic status and geographical features.

● Research a range of health risks and how models may help the understanding of their patterns and trends.

Answers and quick quizzes online

Online ☐

Examiner's summary

✔ Health risks vary from short term to chronic.

✔ Different health risks affect people at different scales.

✔ The epidemiological transition model shows how health risk can change over time.

✔ Health risk can impact individuals and nations.

✔ Health risk can be divided into internal and external causes.

✔ Spatial variations in health can be influenced by socio-economic factors.

✔ Health risk can be affected by both physical and human geographical factors.

✔ The spread of disease can be illustrated by diffusion models.

✔ Environmental health risks can be divided into one-off (incidental) pollution incidents and longer-term (sustained) pollution.

✔ Health risks from incidental pollution and sustained pollution are many and varied.

✔ Kuznets' environmental curve suggests that there is a relationship between environmental quality and economic development.

✔ Pollution fatigue leads to public pressure for action to either manage the incident better or avoid future incidents.

✔ The impacts of health risk can be both short term and long term on both individuals and groups of people.

✔ Some health risks are harder to manage than others.

✔ The WHO is the most important single global advisory health organisation.

✔ Uganda is a country that is having some success in managing some health issues while others are proving more difficult.

13 Consuming the rural landscape — leisure and tourism

The growth of leisure and tourism landscapes

The rise of leisure and tourism
Revised

Leisure is time spent away from work or time that is considered free time. **Recreation** refers to the activities and pursuits that people take part in during leisure time. **Tourism** is when people travel away from their usual place of living for leisure or business reasons and the activities that people participate in during this time away. Figure 13.1 shows the relationship between these three aspects.

> **Examiner's tip**
>
> Make sure you don't get muddled with your definitions — these are an important basis for the understanding required in this option.

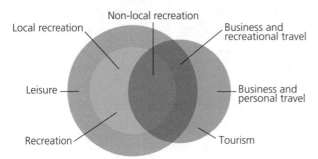

Figure 13.1 The relationship between leisure, recreation and tourism

Leisure and tourism are big business. In 2011 tourism worldwide contributed more than US$1 trillion to the world economy, an increase from US$928 billion in 2010. The number of international tourist arrivals also increased in 2011 to reach 983 million worldwide, up 4.6% from 940 million in 2010. Some of the reasons for this growth in leisure and tourism include:

- more leisure time as people receive more paid holiday from work
- an increase in global wealth, personal incomes and the rise of a global middle class
- improved technology leading to cheaper transport, especially air travel
- an increase in life expectancy and the opportunity for retired people to travel
- increased awareness of exotic and far-away places through television, magazines and the internet

Now test yourself
Tested

1 Explain the meanings of the terms 'leisure', 'recreation' and 'tourism'.
2 Give reasons why the number of global tourists continues to increase.

Answers online

The range of rural landscapes

Revised

Leisure and tourism activities make use of a wide range of rural landscapes for a number of different activities. Many of these activities have seen growth in recent years and a range of types of leisure can be seen in Figure 13.2.

Increasingly natural and less managed → More managed and less natural

Remoter wilderness area	Farmscape and accessible rural	Rural–urban fringe
Wilderness areas are heavily protected against development so leisure and tourism is generally restricted and highly managed. Many locations remain inaccessible and off the beaten track — they are exclusive. Landscape quality is high and often well protected by legislation. Typical activities could include: • wild camping and trails • tourist trails • wildlife spectacles (low key)/tourist gaze, e.g. Antarctica • engaging with local culture, e.g. Masai village, Kenya • sustainable ecotourism in rainforests	More accessible rural areas may be dominated by a post-production agricultural landscape, together with agri-environmental schemes. Large numbers of tourists can be accommodated in honey-pot areas. Car parking and visitor facilities may be common. Examples may include: • organic farms with visitor centre/speciality food shop • tourist accommodation and holiday lets • craft centres • wildlife/'touchy-feely' farms • paint-balling and quad biking • woodland trails (e.g. mountain biking)	Highly accessible rural landscapes (typically rural–urban fringe or urban hinter-land) are often battlegrounds between conservationists, planners and developers. Conflicts may occur over both activities and development, especially near to greenbelts or other specially designated areas: • horse stabling and livery • golf courses • craft shops/farm shops • garden centres/horticulture • barns for small rural enterprise • organic food-box schemes • fish (trout) farming • dog breeding • vineyards

Figure 13.2 Different types of leisure and their location

Now test yourself

Tested

3   Summarise the different types of leisure activity that can take place in different areas.

Answer online

Revision activity

Explain the relationship between the growth of leisure and tourism and the use of the rural landscape.

Attitudes of different groups

Revised

The use of rural landscapes for leisure and tourism leads to a range of attitudes about how the rural landscape should be used:

- **Governments** may act to protect areas of beauty for future generations or choose to designate areas of land for recreation purposes through, for example, the creation of National Parks.

- **Intergovernmental agencies** such as Landscapes for People, Food and Nature promote the integrated management of rural landscapes. The European Landscape Convention promotes the protection, management and planning of European landscapes and organises European cooperation on landscape issues.

- **Businesses** can have a vested interest in how the rural landscape is used, including farmers, loggers, hotel owners and extreme sports companies. Some businesses may wish to protect the landscape, whereas others are more focused on exploiting it for commercial gain.

- **Pressure groups** such as the Campaign to Protect Rural England (CPRE) work to ensure that the British countryside is protected for all to enjoy now and in the future.

- **Communities** are home to groups of people who live in villages or small towns and have a vested interest in how the rural landscape around them is used. Many of these people depend on the rural landscape to earn a living.

- **Individual people**, who have a relationship with the rural landscape — and whether it should be used for commercial or recreational reasons, or a combination of both — often have their own views.

> **Now test yourself**   Tested ☐
>
> 4   Suggest some of the views that different groups of people can have towards the rural landscape.
>
> **Answer online**

> **Examiner's tip**
>
> Make sure all the examples and case studies you use are rural; oceans are not rural and neither are cities or other urban areas.

Conflicts   Revised ☐

The use of rural landscapes for leisure and tourism can create conflict between the different users. For example, in the Lake District National Park in the UK there have been issues regarding the use of boats. Lake Windermere saw the imposition of a 10 nautical miles per hour speed limit in 2005 in order to reduce the conflict between those who want to use the lake for speed boats and those who want to sail at much lower speeds. Other conflicts can arise, such as:

- walkers conflicting with mountain-bike users as they compete for the same tracks

- those seeking peace and quiet in the countryside as opposed to those who wish to use quad bikes

- the problems of increased traffic in National Parks

- footpath erosion and its impact on biodiversity

> **Now test yourself**   Tested ☐
>
> 5   How can the rural landscape lead to conflict between different leisure users?
>
> **Answer online**

The significance and fragility of rural landscapes

Physical significance and ecological value   Revised ☐

Some rural landscapes can be considered to be historically and culturally valuable:

- **ecological and physical value** refers to the condition of the landscape and the attributes and resources that the landscape can offer

- **socio-cultural value** refers to how the landscape contributes to the physical and mental health of people or enhances their wellbeing
- **economic value** refers to the financial value of the land if it were to be sold and the value of activities that could take place there

Tested

6 Describe the ways in which rural landscapes can be considered to be valuable.

Answer online

Revision activity

Explain how rural landscapes are significant in their use for leisure and tourism.

Fragile landscapes
Revised

Rural landscapes can be considered in terms of **fragility**, i.e. how susceptible the landscape is to damage. Some rural landscapes that are high in ecological value may also be considered fragile because any disturbance to them may damage them, perhaps beyond repair. Figure 13.3 illustrates how the fragility of rural landscapes can be determined.

Overall landscape sensitivity and fragility =

Landscape character sensitivity
Based on judgements about sensitivity of:

Natural factors
Vegetation types
Tree cover type/pattern
Extent and pattern of semi-natural habitat

Cultural factors
Land use
Settlement pattern
Field boundaries
Enclosure pattern
Time depth/historical significance

Landscape quality/condition
Intactness
Representation of typical character
State of repair of individual elements

Aesthetic factors
Scale
Enclosure
Diversity
Texture
Pattern
Colour
Form/line
Balance
Movement

+

Visual sensitivity

General visibility
Landform influences
Tree and woodland cover

Population
Numbers and types of residents
Numbers and types of visitors

Mitigation potential
Scope for mitigating potential visual impacts

Figure 13.3 Factors to consider when judging overall landscape sensitivity and fragility

Tested

7 Which factors should be considered when judging overall landscape sensitivity and fragility?

Answer online

Threats to rural landscapes
Revised

Models can be used to determine the degree of threat to rural landscapes:

- The **carrying capacity model** puts forward the notion that a rural landscape can cope only with a limited number of people before the landscape is put at risk of damage. It argues that there is a threshold of people using the landscape, which if exceeded will lead to damage.
- The **resilience model** argues that there is a limit to the ability of a rural landscape to withstand pressure and remain intact and if this is exceeded then damage will occur.

Examiner's tip

Make sure you understand how both carrying capacity and resilience can be used to determine the degree of threat to your selected case studies.

Now test yourself
Tested

8 Explain the terms 'carrying capacity model' and 'resilience model' in relation to rural landscapes.

Answer online

Qualitative and quantitative measures
Revised

It is possible to use both qualitative and quantitative methods to measure the quality of rural environments:

- **Qualitative methods** are those that are subjective and do not rely on statistical or numerical data. Such methods may refer to the 'look' and 'feel' of the rural landscape and can be assessed through photographs, field sketches, environmental impact assessments and interviews.
- **Quantitative methods** are those that rely on hard numerical data and statistics, such as counting the types of species of plants that exist in a landscape or the number of visitors who use the area.

Now test yourself

9 Describe a range of qualitative and quantitative methods that could be used to determine if a rural landscape should be protected.

Answer online

Tested

Impact on rural landscapes

Negative impacts
Revised

There is a range of negative impacts that leisure and tourism activities can have on rural landscapes, including:

- **trampling** — the number of walkers over time can damage the rural landscape by wandering from designated footpaths
- **pollution** — through air pollution from the build-up of large numbers of vehicles, particularly during the peak holiday season, as well as water pollution and littering
- **erosion** — from many uses such as walking, mountain biking and quad biking, all of which can lead to the erosion of both designated footpaths and surface rocks
- **habitat disturbance** — people using the rural landscape unwittingly disturb the natural environment of plants and animals

Now test yourself

10 Describe some of the negative impacts that leisure and tourism activities can have on rural landscapes.

Answer online

Tested

Positive impacts Revised

There is a range of positive impacts that leisure and tourism activities can have on rural landscapes, including:

- **wildlife conservation** — wildlife and the landscape itself are encouraged to be protected and conserved, both for the enjoyment of visitors and for the people who live there
- **river restoration** — organisations such as the River Restoration Centre (RRC) work to promote, facilitate and support best practice in river, watercourse and floodplain management in rural landscapes across the UK
- **conservation of heritage sites** — England's National Parks contain over 63 300 listed buildings, more than 10 400 nationally important ancient monuments and some 300 designated historic parks and gardens

Now test yourself

11 Describe some of the positive impacts that leisure and tourism activities can have on rural landscapes.

Answer online

Tested

Changing impacts Revised

The impact of human use on the rural landscape can change over time, depending on the way in which the landscape is used. For example, National Parks in the UK have moved beyond being passive landscapes that people used to visit to enjoy quiet solitude; now they are much more 'active' areas as people use them for extreme sports activities such as hang-gliding, paragliding and mountain biking.

Examiner's tip

Research a National Park and consider the impacts of human use of the park over time as a case study in your exam.

Now test yourself

Tested

12 Suggest ways in which the impact of human activities on rural landscapes can change over time.

Answer online

Revision activity

Describe the range of impacts that leisure and tourism can have on rural landscapes.

Threats and opportunities Revised

Globally, as more people see an increase in their disposable income, **tourism hotspots** are experiencing increasing numbers of visitors. This can have both positive and negative impacts for the rural landscape. Table 13.1 shows how the television and film industries have opened up the appeal of rural landscapes to visitors.

Table 13.1 Examples of television programmes and films that have promoted the rural landscape

UK locations	
The Wicker Man (1973)	Dumfries and Galloway
Harry Potter series (2001–11)	Alnwick Castle, Northumberland
Pride and Prejudice (2005)	The Peak District
International locations	
Star Wars (1977)	Chott el Djerid, Tunisia
A Passage to India (1984)	Marabar Caves, nr Chandrapore, rural India
The Beach (2000)	Phi Phi Islands, Thailand
The Lord of the Rings series (2001–03)	Kaitoke Regional Park, New Zealand
Narnia series (2005–present)	Table Mountains, Poland; New Zealand
Brokeback Mountain (2005)	Alberta, Canada
Honeypots for rural tourism	
Television also establishes honeypots for rural tourism. Balamory is a children's show that began filming in 2002 on the Scottish island of Mull, which subsequently experienced an influx of tiny tourists (accompanied by their parents). Heartbeat's rural set locations in Yorkshire have also become popular with tourists.	

Now test yourself

Tested ☐

13 How have the television and film industries opened up the appeal of rural landscapes?

Answer online

Rural landscape management issues

Whether rural landscapes should be managed or not

Revised ☐

There is a wide range of ways of managing the rural landscape, from total protection to total exploitation. Figure 13.4 shows these views as a continuum.

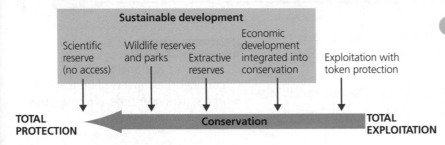

Now test yourself

14 Summarise the approaches that exist for managing rural landscapes.

Answer online

Tested ☐

Figure 13.4 The spectrum of ways in which rural landscapes can be managed

Management strategies

Revised ☐

A number of management strategies can be used to manage rural landscapes, including:

- **preservation** — keeping the environment in its natural state with minimal human use allowed. It can also apply to historic buildings or landmarks that make up the rural landscape

- **conservation** — more active management to protect the rural landscape through particular policies, actions or initiatives, often alongside human use of the area

- **stewardship** — responsible planning and actions in order to maintain and enhance working rural landscapes. The Scottish Rural Stewardship Scheme was set up to provide assistance to encourage farmers to adopt environmentally friendly practices

- **sustainable management** — the rural landscape is managed in order that it can be enjoyed by people now as well as by generations in the future. This approach often involves ensuring local people can continue to make a living in the area

- the **growth of ecotourism** — people travel to remote and pristine rural landscapes with the intention of causing minimal damage to the environment. Such tourism often involves an element of conservation

Mitigation strategies are used to lessen the impact of tourists to rural areas, such as using natural materials to repair footpaths and walkways to prevent erosion.

Revision activity

Explain how rural landscapes used for leisure and tourism can be managed.

Attitudes and strategies of different groups Revised ☐

Different users of the rural landscape often have conflicting attitudes about how rural landscapes should be used. You should be aware of the attitudes of different groups towards the located case studies that you have researched for the exam and will need to consider the following points:

- What are the views of the residents or people who live in the rural landscape?
- What role (if any) does the government play in the preservation or conservation of the landscape?
- What pressure groups exist and how are they affecting the use of the landscape?
- What are the interests of business and industry?

Examiner's tip

It is useful to produce a conflict matrix to determine the extent of conflict that exists between different groups for the case studies and examples that you have chosen to research.

Different approaches Revised ☐

There are a number of approaches for managing rural environments and some are more effective than others. Table 13.2 suggests a number of management approaches that can be adopted in rural areas.

Table 13.2 Approaches to the management of rural landscapes

Direct	Indirect
Often used in most fragile areas or in a potentially dangerous situation, e.g. waterfall, crumbling ruin	Usually more successful and cheaper in remoter locations
Most time-consuming and expensive	Seeks to affect behaviour through education, information and persuasion
May need to start with this in the short term to protect, moving on to more indirect means as education kicks in	Visitors can be informed about the impacts connected with a certain activity or given information that encourages the use of certain areas over threatened areas
Regulations may entail enforcement, restricting activities or rationing use	May involve physical alteration such as the redirection of a trail to a more resilient area of a forest, influencing the movement of visitors
Hard, e.g. paths, fences, vegetation clearance, reseeding	Soft, e.g. land-use zoning, litter bins, interpretation signs and centres, nature trails

Tested

Now test yourself

18 Explain the ways in which rural landscapes can be managed.

Answer online

Exam practice

Report-style essay

'The use of rural landscapes for leisure and tourism is more controversial in some areas than others.' Discuss. [70]

Pre-released research focus

● Explore the impacts of leisure and tourism as a consumer of rural landscapes and the role of their management.

● Research a range of locations showing differing impacts from recreational and tourism users.

Answers and quick quizzes online

Online

Examiner's summary

✔ Leisure and tourism is a large and growing global industry.

✔ There is a range of rural landscapes with a wide range of leisure and tourism opportunities.

✔ The use of rural landscapes for leisure and tourism can lead to a range of different attitudes from different groups.

✔ The use of rural landscapes for leisure and tourism can create conflicts between different users.

✔ Some rural landscapes can be considered to be historically or culturally valuable.

✔ Rural landscapes are fragile and susceptible to damage.

✔ The carrying capacity model and the resilience model can be used to determine the degree of threat to rural landscapes.

✔ Both qualitative and quantitative methods can be used to measure the quality of rural environments and their usefulness.

✔ There is a range of negative impacts that leisure and tourism activities can have on rural landscapes.

✔ There is a range of positive impacts that leisure and tourism activities can have on rural landscapes.

✔ The impact of human use on the rural landscape can change over time, depending on the way in which the landscape is used.

✔ Tourism hotspots are experiencing increasing numbers of visitors as more people see a rise in their disposable income.

✔ There is a range of arguments for and against the management of rural landscapes, from total protection to total exploitation.

✔ There is a range of management strategies that can be used to manage rural landscapes.

✔ Different users of the rural landscape have conflicting attitudes about ways in which the landscape can and should be used.

✔ There is a range of different approaches to managing rural environments.